TALKING TO GOD

"THY KINGDOM COME!

THY WILL BE DONE!

ON EARTH AS IT IS IN HEAVEN."

This book is dedicated
to the Teachers and Children
of B. F. E. S. School,
Herford, Germany,
and the Holy Family School,
Langley,
who inspired so much of it.

Thanks are due to those
who have made helpful suggestions,
especially Father David Konstant.

TALKING TO GOD

BY

J. R. McCLORRY

ST PAUL PUBLICATIONS

ST PAUL PUBLICATIONS,
Langley, Bucks. — England.

ST PAUL PUBLICATIONS,
Ballykeeran, Athlone — Ireland.

NIHIL OBSTAT
E. Hardwick, *Censor Deputatus*

IMPRIMATUR
Gerardus Collins, *Vicarius Generalis*
Northantoniae, die 2a januarii 1967.

Printed in Great Britain by the Society of St Paul, Langley, Slough.

CONTENTS

INTRODUCTION

In compiling this book I have been motivated by various factors, not the least of which, is the absolute necessity of educating our children in a life of prayer which must never become a life of meaningless repetition of vocal prayers.

Naturally, a school assembly uses vocal forms, but the aim is always to point to the mystery behind the reading and to crystallize it in a prayer. In this context, one should not forget the value of silent prayer—30 seconds are usually enough for Primary children.

A school assembly should be a corporate act of worship and this means that the children and the teachers should take an active part and that both teachers and children should face the school altar or crucifix.

Normally a child should do the reading. In fact, a child or group of children could compose and lead a whole assembly under the inspiration of the class teacher.

The atmosphere of the Assembly is set by its beginning, and music—either a gramophone or piano—helps the atmosphere.

On occasions, a recorder group could accompany the hymn. Such a group from a backward class can learn a simple hymn tune.

The Assembly themes, readings and prayers which follow, are obviously not exhaustive. They can be divided into three terms, and each takes note of the Liturgical cycle and of Feast Days.

My hope is that this book will not be used as *the* aid to be followed day by day, but that it will provide a stimulus to many teachers to draw up many similar themes to use in their own schools.

The children used for the readings have been generally third or fourth year Juniors, but in June and July, we have used better readers from the second year Juniors.

1

Hymns, since they are prayers, should have words suited to the age of the children who sing them and therefore, many from present hymn books should not be used for Primary children. Much use could be made of chants, e.g. Gelineau Psalms. Suggestions for hymns have not been made—but there is no school hymnal really suited to Primary School needs. Search widely and use the most suitable you can find.

This type of Assembly has been introduced into a school having a very indifferent assembly and into a completely new school; its effect on the children has, I feel, been such that it has helped them to think of what they are doing, and thoughts and ideas and examples seep into their minds gradually and become part and parcel of themselves so that they will have thoughts to think of in their joys and sorrows outside of any set prayer time. And most of it is from the Word of God Himself, from the Bible, which is our rich heritage.

This book, then, is offered as a contribution to thought on our school assemblies as a means of forming the prayer life of our children and as an aid to the busy teacher in preparing the most important act in the school day.

The form of Assembly is that generally favoured by Canon Drinkwater:

  (i)   Theme.

 (ii)   Sign of the cross and opening invocation.

(iii)   Hymn.

(iv)   Reading.

 (v)   Prayer.

(vi)   The Lord's Prayer.

(vii)   Blessing.

(viii)   The Souls in purgatory. (*Occasionally.*)

(ix)   Sign of the Cross.

A child or group of children can take the whole Assembly. If, however, it is thought desirable to have a teacher in charge, it is suggested that the child at least do the Reading and say the Prayer.

1. FOR THE BEGINNING OF THE SCHOOL YEAR

V. Blessed be the Holy and Undivided Trinity.
R. Now and for evermore. Amen.

HYMN

READING

We have just enjoyed our long summer holiday and should be ready and refreshed for a good term's work.

Now, perhaps, we should begin by reminding ourselves that God made us for a very special reason. He made us to know Him, to love Him and to serve Him.

We will get to know him if we give ourselves to Him by paying attention during the religious lesson, if we go to Mass and Holy Communion regularly and if we say our prayers without fail.

We will show Him that we love Him by doing everything for him. By everything we mean all that we think, or say, or do. We mean that we offer Him not only our prayers, Masses and Communions but also our reading, our painting, arithmetic, games, songs, friendships, errands. All these things we can offer to Our Lord and we should offer them to Him each morning when we make our Morning Offering during our morning prayers, which we say before we come to school. In this way all that we think, or say, or do, will be for the love of God and will keep us very close to Him all through the day.

We serve God best by doing what He wants us to do at any time. Just now he wants us to do our work in school. We will promise Him, then, that we will do our best in this during this school year. Don't forget that God has a special way for everyone to serve Him and your teachers know that they are serving Him by teaching you and they will be telling Our Lord that they will be doing all that they can for you because that is what Our Lord wants of them.

Let us think for a little while to ourselves about what we have just heard and tell Our Lord in our own way all that we will try to do for Him.

Welcome (*Short pause for about half a minute for silent prayer.*)

Jesus, Mary and Joseph, make our school a happy school and a holy one.

PRAYER

Lord bless our school so that by working together and playing together we may learn to love one another and to serve You, through Jesus Christ our Lord. Amen.

THE LORD'S PRAYER   *Ask help of*
Hymn - Guardian Angel.

BLESSING

May the God, who gives us life and love, help us to see Him in the beauty of His wonderful creation and find Him in all the ways of happiness today and every day. Amen.
May the souls of the faithful departed, through the mercy of God, rest in peace. Amen.

2.   FOR KINDNESS

V. Lord, open my lips!
R. And my mouth will declare your praise.

Glory be to the Father, and to the Son and to the Holy Spirit.
As it was in the beginning, is now, and ever shall be, world without end. Amen.

HYMN

READING

Never tell lies. We should all tell the truth always to our neighbour. We are all Christians. If someone hurts

4

us by unkind words or deeds we should not be angry at him. We should not let any day end and still be angry. Do not let the devil have any chance!

If we have ever stolen we should make up our minds never to steal again. If we work hard we will have no excuse to steal. We should share what we have with others especially with those who are in need.

Do not talk about anything you would not say to your mother or to Our Blessed Lady. Let all you have to say be a good example to others and bring grace to them. We all belong to God and share in His Life and His Love because we have been baptised.

We should not be quarrelsome or say unkind or spiteful things or tell tales about others. Be kind and tender to one another. Be generous to everybody as God in Christ has been generous to you.

PRAYER

O God, help us to love You with all our heart and to love our neighbour, for your sake. Fill our hearts with love and kindness, so that by always being happy at the success of others, by feeling with them when they are sad, by never thinking anything evil, we may become more like you who are the true and perfect love. We ask this through Jesus Christ, your Son, who lives and reigns with you and the Holy Spirit for ever and ever, world without end. Amen.

THE LORD'S PRAYER

BLESSING

May the Lord give us every help to forgive those who have harmed us in any way. May He give us a pure mind and sincere love of our neighbours, through Jesus Christ our Lord. Amen.

And may the souls of the faithful departed, through the mercy of God, rest in peace. Amen.

3. PRAISE THE LORD!

V. Lord, open my lips!

R. And my mouth will declare your praise.

Glory be to the Father and to the Son and to the Holy Spirit. As it was in the beginning, is now, and ever shall be, world without end. Amen.

HYMN

READING

Praise the Lord!
Praise the Lord from the heavens,
   praise him in the heights!
Praise him, all his angels,
   praise him, all his host!
Praise him, sun and moon,
   praise him, all you shining stars!
Praise him, you highest heavens,
   and you waters above the heavens!
Let them praise the name of the Lord!
   For he commanded and they were created.
And he established them for ever and ever;
   he fixed their bounds which cannot be passed.
Praise the Lord from the earth,
   you sea monsters and all deeps,
Fire and hail, snow and frost,
   stormy wind fulfilling his command!
Mountains and all hills,
   fruit trees and all cedars!
Beasts and all cattle,
   creeping things and flying birds!
Kings of the earth and all peoples,
   princes and all rulers of the earth!
Young men and maidens together,
   old men and children!
Let them praise the name of the Lord.

PRAYER

Dear Lord, help us to praise you today by our thoughts. May we often think of you. May we praise you in all our work and all our play, so that whatever we do may glorify your name. May we praise you in our words so that what we have to say may bring us closer to you, our Lord and our God who lives and reigns now and always. Amen.

THE LORD'S PRAYER

BLESSING

May the blessing of God the Father, God the Son and God the Holy Spirit be with us now and always. Amen.

May the souls of the faithful departed, through the mercy of God, rest in peace. Amen.

4.   FIRST FRIDAYS

V. Most Sacred Heart of Jesus, we implore.

R. That we may ever love you more and more.

HYMN

READING

On each first Friday of every month we think especially of the Sacred Heart of Jesus. This is a way of thinking of God's great love for us. When we want to tell our mother or someone how very much we love them the best way we can think of saying this is to say that we love them with all our heart.

God our Father loves us so much that He sent His own Son, Jesus, to show us how to love Him. Jesus came to give us a share of God's life and God's love, and to teach us the way to our Father. Jesus loves us so much. How terrible it is to love someone if they do not love you back! Not many people loved Jesus although he was so good and so kind. They crucified Him.

Often we say "No" to what God wants and we pay back all Jesus' love by not loving him back.

Today we should think of all that Jesus has done for us and try in some little way to make up for not loving Him enough. We can try, too, to make up for all the wickedness of all those who hate Him. Think of one way in which you can do this today—perhaps by some extra prayer of love or by saying "No" to yourself in some way. The best way if you can manage it is to go to Mass and Holy Communion.

(Pause for about half a minute to think about this.)

Now we will say an act of Consecration to the Sacred Heart.

Most Sacred Heart of Jesus, You told Saint Margaret Mary that you would give special blessings to those who honoured Your Sacred Heart. We want to give our hearts and lives to You.

We want to do this especially because of Your great love for us. You came down from heaven and lived so as to teach us how to please God our Father. When people would not listen to You, You died for us and rose again, to teach us that, if only we would obey our Father, You would one day lead us to be with You, and to be happy with You forever in Your Heavenly Kingdom.

We offer our love to You also to try to make up for all the times we have said "No" to what God wants of us, and because in this way we have been so unlike You who showed us that we should always do the Will of our Father.

Lastly, we offer ourselves to You to try to make up for all those who are wicked and who will not listen to what You want of them. We offer ourselves to You to make up for all the selfishness there is. Most Sacred Heart of Jesus, we make this offering through our Blessed Lady and Saint Joseph who loved You so much. Help us to love You. Bless and protect us and our homes and school.

Most Sacred Heart of Jesus, we put all our trust in You. Take our offering and help us to follow Your example. Amen.

BLESSING

May the peace of God which passes all our understanding keep our hearts and minds in the knowledge and the love of Christ Jesus our Lord. Amen.

5. SUFFER LITTLE CHILDREN

V. O God, come to my assistance!

R. O Lord, make haste to help me.

Glory be to the Father, and to the Son and to the Holy Spirit.
As it was in the beginning, is now, and ever shall be, world
without end. Amen.

HYMN

READING

The reading is from the Good News told by St.
Matthew.

"Then children were brought to him that he might
lay his hands on them and pray. The disciples rebuked
the people; but Jesus said, 'Let the children come to me,
and do not hinder them; for to such belongs the kingdom of heaven.' And he laid his hands on them and went
away."

PRAYER

Dear Jesus, we know that you love us. Teach us always to love
you. Help us always to be obedient, honest, truthful and pure.
Give us the grace to put your ways and your example before everything else so that we may always be worthy to come to you. May
we at last share with you the everlasting joys of heaven. Amen.

THE LORD'S PRAYER

BLESSING

May the God of peace sanctify us and may our minds, our souls
and our bodies be kept without sin ready for the coming again of
Our Lord Jesus Christ. Amen.

6. THE POOR

HYMN

READING

Listen today to part of Psalm 41.

"Blessed is he who considers the poor!
  The Lord delivers him in the day of trouble;
  the Lord protects him and keeps him alive;
      he is called blessed in the land;
  The Lord sustains him on his sickbed;
      in his illness thou healest all his infirmities.
  By this I know that thou art pleased with me.
  Blessed be the Lord, the God of Israel,
      from everlasting to everlasting!
      Amen and Amen."

PRAYER

O God, our Father, let us always feel for those in need. Let us always hate greediness and try to help those who are poor in whatever way we can. We ask this in the name of the friend of the poor, Jesus Christ your Son who lives and reigns with you in the unity of the Holy Spirit, world without end. Amen.

THE LORD'S PRAYER

BLESSING

Jesus, you were born poor in a stable in Bethlehem. Bless today all the poor people and all those who are suffering in any way and may we too share in your blessing.

7. COME TO ME

V. I have lifted up my eyes to the hills!

R. From whence my help shall come.

V. My help comes from the Lord.

R. Who made heaven and earth.

Glory be to the Father. . . .

HYMN

READING

Sometimes things seem to go wrong for us. Sometimes it seems hard to be good. Sometimes perhaps we feel as though we can't be bothered to try or even to say our prayers. Listen then to what our Lord has to say to us at the end of Chapter XI in St. Matthew's Gospel. It is so short that we can easily remember it and when we feel like that we can say it to ourselves:

"Come to me, all who labour and are heavy laden, and I will give you rest.

Take my yoke upon you and learn from me;

For I am gentle and lowly in heart,

And you will find rest for your souls."

PRAYER

Teach us, Lord, always to find rest in you by doing always what you want us to do. Teach us to pray often and to think often of the lessons and examples you gave us and to say well the best of all prayers which you taught us yourself: Our Father . . .

BLESSING

The Lord bless us and keep us. The Lord help us to understand and may He fill us with faith and love towards Him. May the Lord be with us in our coming out and our going in and may he at last bring us to His everlasting peace for Jesus Christ's sake. Amen.

8. SERVE THE LORD WITH GLADNESS

V. Lord, open my lips!
R. And my mouth will declare your praise!
   Glory be to the Father. . . .

HYMN

READING

Today's reading is one of the great songs from the Holy
Bible. It is Psalm 100.
  "Make a joyful noise to the Lord, all the lands!
    Serve the Lord with gladness!
    Come into his presence with singing!
  Know that the Lord is God!
    It is he that made us and we are his;
    we are his people, and the sheep of his pasture.
  Enter his gates with thanksgiving,
    and his courts with praise!
    Give thanks to him, bless his name!
  For the Lord is good;
    his steadfast love endures for ever,
    and his faithfulness to all generations."

PRAYER

Let us always and with a gladsome mind praise the Lord, for He is
good. Let us today praise Him for His kindness, for His mercies
and for His forgiveness of all our wrongdoings. Let us offer Him
today and forever all our thoughts, words and actions, so that no
thought, word or deed may ever again offend Him. Now we will
say these things to God our Father in the quiet of our own minds.

(Pause for about half a minute.)

THE LORD'S PRAYER

BLESSING

May we grow in grace and in the knowledge of our Lord and
Saviour Jesus Christ to whom be glory and honour both now and
forever more. Amen.

9. JUDGE NOT

V. Show us Lord your mercy!
R. And grant us your salvation.
V. Lord, hear my prayer.
R. And let my cry come to you.

HYMN

READING

Sometimes we think too easily that other people are wrong and we often blame them for things when we don't really know all about it. Listen to what our Lord says in the Good News told by St. Matthew.

"Judge not, that you be not judged. Why do you see the speck that is in your brother's eye, but do not notice the log that is in your own eye? Or how can you say to your brother, 'Let me take the speck out of your eye,' when there is the log in your own eye? You hypocrite! First take the log out of your own eye, and then you will see clearly to take the speck out of your brother's eye."

PRAYER

Dear Lord, help us to keep from the sin of judging others hastily and from blaming them in our own thoughts and actions. Help us to be kind to all those who may offend us today and to remember that we ourselves are not perfect. Pardon our offences, and help us to be more like you in all that we think or say or do, for your name's sake. Amen.

THE LORD'S PRAYER

BLESSING

Shine your light in our hearts, O God, and guide us in the way that leads to everlasting happiness with you, for Jesus Christ's sake. Amen.

10. THE SICK MAN ON THE HOUSE TOP

V. Blessed be the Holy and Undivided Trinity!
R. Now and for evermore. Amen.

HYMN

READING

The reading today is from the Good News told by St. Mark. It shows how Jesus looks after our souls as well as our bodies. It tells us that it is more important to have a healthy soul than a healthy body.

"And when he returned to Capernaum after some days, it was reported that he was at home. And many were gathered together, so that there was no longer room for them not even about the door; and he was preaching the word to them. And they came, bringing to him a paralytic carried by four men. And when they could not get near him because of the crowd, they removed the roof above him; and when they had made an opening, they let down the pallet on which the paralytic lay. And when Jesus saw their faith, he said to the paralytic, 'My son, your sins are forgiven.' Now some of the scribes were sitting there, questioning in their hearts, 'Why does this man speak thus? It is blasphemy! Who can forgive sins but God alone?' And immediately Jesus, perceiving in his spirit that they thus questioned within themselves, said to them, 'Why do you question thus in your hearts? Which is easier, to say to the paralytic, "Your sins are forgiven," or to say, "Rise, take up your pallet and walk"? But that you may know that the Son of man has authority on earth to forgive sins'—he said to the paralytic—'I say to you, rise, take up your pallet and go home.' And he rose, and immediately took up the pallet and went out before them all; so that they were all amazed and glorified God, saying, 'We never saw anything like this!' "

PRAYER

Lord, we believe in you. We know that you can forgive sins and that you can help the sick. Please help all sinners to be really sorry for their sins. Help us to be sorry for our sins so that all people may love you more and more. Our Blessed Lady, you loved God so much that you never said "No" to Him. Pray for us sinners now and at the hour of our death. Amen.

THE LORD'S PRAYER

BLESSING

May the blessing of God Almighty, the Father, the Son and the Holy Spirit be with us and remain with us this day and for evermore. Amen.

11. FOR THOSE WHO WORK ON THE LAND

V. I have lifted up my eyes to the hills!
R. From whence my help comes.
V. My help comes from the Lord.
R. Who made heaven and earth.

    Glory be to the Father. . . .

HYMN

READING

One of the things we all need is Food. Children who live in the country and who see the cattle in the fields know that they need a lot of looking after. They have to be fed and looked after. Men and women have to get up early to feed them and milk them. They have to be fed and milked every day of the week and every week of the year. It is hard work that has to be done also in winter—even on the coldest day.

The shepherd who looks after the sheep and lambs has a hard life. The lambs are usually born near the end of winter or early spring when it is cold. There is often snow on the hills. The shepherd has to go out in all weathers and is often lonely. Sheep are often silly and stupid animals. The shepherd has to be very patient with them and his work is not easy.

There is a great deal to do working on the land. There is ploughing, sowing, hoeing, gathering in the harvest looking after all the farm machinery. This is very hard work which goes on every day whatever the weather.

All those who work on the land are really working for us. Many of us may never really have seen a farm but we all eat bread and cakes and meat and butter. We eat potatoes and other vegetables. We wear clothes made from wool. These things all come from farms, from people who work hard on the land.

We should thank God for these things which He gives us and pray often for those who work so hard so that we can share God's gifts to us.

PRAYER

Today, Lord, we want to pray for all those who work on the land. Grant that they may see you in the good earth, in the seed and in the growing crops. We join them in giving thanks to you for all your goodness to us all. Bless them in their work. Help them when it is hard. Guard and protect them always. Amen.

THE LORD'S PRAYER

BLESSING

O God, may your blessing rest upon us, and all that we do in your Name, for Jesus Christ's sake. Amen.

16

12. HARVEST THANKSGIVING

Gifts are placed on and around the altar before prayers begin.

V. For all fruits and vegetables,
R. We thank you Lord.

V. For all meat and drink,
R. We thank you Lord.

V. For our clothing and houses,
R. We thank you Lord.

V. For giving men the power to make wonderful machines,
R. We thank you Lord.

V. For all your great goodness to us,
R. We thank you Lord.

HYMN

READING

When God had saved the Israelites from Egypt and given them the Promised Land He spoke to Moses and told him that the Israelites were to give thanks for the harvest as we read in the book of Leviticus:

"When you have gathered in the produce of the land, you shall keep the feast of the Lord seven days; on the first day shall be a solemn rest, and on the eighth day shall be a solemn rest. And you shall take on the first day the fruit of goodly trees, branches of palm trees, and boughs of leafy trees, and willows of the brook; and you shall rejoice before the Lord your God seven days. You shall keep it as a feast to the Lord seven days in the year."

A token number of further gifts may now be brought to the altar.
The children sit.

PRAYER

either

V. Blessed are You, O Lord the God of our Fathers
R. And worthy to be praised, and glorious for ever.

V. Let us bless the Father and the Son with the Holy Ghost
R. Let us praise and exult Him above all for ever.

V. Blessed are You, O Lord in the firmament of Heaven.
R. And worthy to be praised and glorious, and exalted above all for ever.

V. O Lord hear my prayer
R. And let my cry come to You.

Let Us Pray

O God, Your mercies are without number, and the treasure of Your goodness is infinite. We thank You for all Your gifts of the Harvest which You have given us. May we be always thankful for them and never waste them: Through Jesus Christ our Lord. Amen.

or

Representatives from each class may read prayers of thanksgiving for the Harvest which they have composed.

BLESSING

Now to the King of ages, immortal, invisible, the only God, be honour and glory for ever and ever. Amen.

The Harvest gifts may later be given to the poor, to old people, auctioned to parents and friends and the proceeds sent to War on Want, etc. Thus the children see how they can help others in a practical way. If the gifts are given to old people, etc., some children should go with a teacher and actually give them. Letters of thanks should later be read out to the children.

13. TRUST IN THE LORD

V. Our help is in the name of the Lord.
R. Who made heaven and earth.
   I confess, to Almighty God. . . .

HYMN

READING

In the reading today we have some very good advice from the book of Proverbs. When we hear these readings we should remember that one of the chief ways God wants to speak to us is through His words in the bible. We should listen to these words very carefully, then, because it is really God giving us a message.

"Do not forget my teaching,
   but let your heart keep my commandments;
Let not loyalty and faithfulness forsake you;
So you will find favour and good repute
   in the sight of God and man.
Trust in the Lord with all your heart,
   and do not rely on your own insight.
In all your ways acknowledge him,
   and he will make straight your paths.
Be not wise in your own eyes
   Love the Lord and turn away from evil."

PRAYER

Dear Lord, we do not know what may be in store for us today. Whatever happens, whether it seems good or bad, we know that it can be used for our good if only we will trust in you. We will try to do your will in all things. Help us to do this for the sake of Jesus Christ your Son who lives and reigns with you in the unity of the Holy Spirit, world without end. Amen.

THE LORD'S PRAYER

BLESSING

May the God of Peace make us holy and may our spirits, our souls and our bodies be kept without sin until the coming of our Lord Jesus Christ. Amen.

14. THE PHARISEE AND THE PUBLICAN

V. O God, come to my help.
R. O Lord, make haste to help me!
Glory be to the Father. . . .

HYMN

READING

Today, St. Luke tells us about two men who said their prayers. It is easy to see which one pleases our Lord the more. I think that sometimes our prayers are more like those of the Pharisee. Listen carefully to what St. Luke says.

"Two men went up into the temple to pray, one a Pharisee and the other a tax collector. The Pharisee stood and prayed thus with himself, 'God, I thank thee that I am not like other men, cheaters and liars, or even like this tax collector. I fast twice a week, I give money to the poor.' But the tax collector, standing far off, would not even lift up his eyes to heaven, but beat his breast, saying, 'God, be merciful to me a sinner!' I tell you, this man went down to his house more pleasing to God than the other; for every one who exalts himself will be humbled but he who humbles himself will be exalted."

PRAYER

Jesus, when you were on earth you gave us an example of how to live in love and humility. Help us to learn from you. Help us to try to do what you would like us to do. Make us humble and sorry for our sins for your sake because you lived and died for us. Amen.

THE LORD'S PRAYER

BLESSING

May God be merciful to us and bless us and give us the grace to know what He wants of us and the strength to do it. We ask this for the sake of Jesus Christ your Son, who lives and reigns with you in the unity of the Holy Spirit, world without end. Amen.

20

15. THE CHARIOT OF FIRE

HYMN

READING

The great prophet Elijah had spent a long and a hard life working for God. He had never been afraid to do what God wanted of him because he trusted God. He knew that God would always help him. Sometimes he had to go and tell the king how much he was displeasing God. Sometimes he had to tell wicked people that they would be punished for their sins and then he had to go away and hide. He trusted in the Spirit of God who was with him. When he was old and ready to die he was taken up into heaven. You will probably remember too, that when Our Lord was transfigured on the mountain the Apostles who were with Him saw Him speaking with Moses and Elijah.

"When they had crossed, Elijah said to Elisha, 'Ask what I shall do for you, before I am taken from you.' And Elisha said, 'I pray you, let me inherit a double share of your spirit.' And he said 'You have asked a hard thing; yet, if you see me as I am being taken from you it shall be so for you; but if you do not see me, it shall not be so.' And as they still went on and talked, behold, a chariot of fire and horses of fire separated the two of them. And Elijah went up by a whirlwind into heaven. And Elisha saw it and cried, 'My father, my father! the chariots of Israel and its horsemen!' And he saw him no more."

PRAYER

O Lord, help us to serve you well by doing our best in our lessons in this school. May we serve you so well that at last with Elijah, and Our blessed Lady and all the saints we may also enjoy being with You forever in heaven. Through Jesus Christ our Lord. Amen.

THE LORD'S PRAYER

BLESSING

May the Lord bless our going out and our coming in from this time forth and forever more. Amen.

16. GOD THE PROVIDER

V. I have lifted up my eyes to the hills.
R. From whence comes my help.
V. My help comes from the Lord.
R. Who made heaven and earth.
Glory be to the Father....

HYMN

READING

Psalm 104 tells us of the wonders of God's creation. Let us listen to some of it and hear about God's great love for us in the works of his creation:

"From thy lofty abode thou waterest the mountains;
 the earth is satisfied with the fruit of thy work.
Thou dost cause the grass to grow for the cattle,
 and plants for man to cultivate,
that he may bring forth food from the earth,
 and wine to gladden the heart of man,
oil to make his face shine,
 and bread to strengthen man's heart.
The trees of the Lord are watered abundantly,
 the cedars of Lebanon which he planted.
In them the birds build their nests;
 the stork has her home in the fir trees.
The high mountains are for the wild goats;
 the rocks are a refuge for the badgers.

Thou hast made the moon to mark the seasons;
   the sun knows its time for setting.
Thou makest darkness, and it is night,
   when all the beasts of the forest creep forth.
The young lions roar for their prey,
   seeking their food from God.
When the sun rises, they get them away
   and lie down in their dens.
Man goes forth to his work
   and to his labour until the evening.
O Lord, how manifold are thy works!
   In wisdom hast thou made them all;
   the earth is full of thy creatures."

PRAYER

Lord, You are all powerful and all mighty. You are the giver of all good things. Help us to be truly thankful for your wonderful creation and to use all the good things you have given us properly. In this way, too, we will be praising and thanking you.

THE LORD'S PRAYER

BLESSING

Give us a heart to praise you, O God, and lips to praise you for all the wonderful things we see around us for Jesus Christ's sake. Amen.

17. DAVID AND JONATHAN

V. O God come to my assistance!
R. O Lord, make haste to help me!
   Glory be to the Father. . . .

HYMN

READING

David the shepherd boy, who was chosen by God to become a great king came to King Saul's palace after he had fought bravely in battle. The King was jealous of David's bravery but the king's son, Jonathan, became his very good friend. He often helped David when Saul was angry with him. Let us listen to the story of this friendship.

"When he had finished speaking to Saul, the soul of Jonathan was knit to the soul of David, and Jonathan loved him as his own soul. And Saul took him that day, and would not let him return to his father's house. Then Jonathan made a promise to David, because he loved him as his own soul. And Jonathan stripped himself of the robe that was upon him, and gave it to David, and his armour, and even his sword and his bow and his girdle."

PRAYER

Lord, help us to be thankful for our friends. Please do not let us be selfish towards them but help us to serve them well. We ask this because we know that you have told us that it is a better thing to give than to receive. Bless us and bless all our friends in all that we do, through Jesus Christ our Lord. Amen.

THE LORD'S PRAYER

BLESSING

May the Lord take us and our friends into his care and keeping this day. May His peace come to our hearts now and stay there always.

18. SAINT MICHAEL

V. Blessed be the holy and undivided Trinity!
R. Now and for evermore. Amen.

THEME

Today is the feast of Saint Michael, one of God's great Angels.

An angel is a spirit who lives with God. Angels are higher than men. They have no bodies and can understand many things which we cannot understand.

God our Father so loved us that He sent His Son to die for us and to help us to take our place in His Heavenly Kingdom. But our Father in Heaven has also given to each of us a special angel to guard us and to help us.

Our angels will help us when we are tempted to do something which will displease God. We should often ask them to help us. When we find it hard to say our prayers, our angels will help us to talk to God more easily if only we will ask them. They will help us always to think good thoughts and to keep close to God.

From the time we are born to the time we die our guardian angel is with us. When we die our angel will take our soul to God.

We should often pray to our Guardian Angel. Each morning and each night we should say the prayer we have learned to our Guardian Angel. During the day we should sometimes talk to our Angel and ask him to look after us.

PRAYER

Saint Michael, we trust that you will help us when we pray that we may really mean what we say in our prayers. Then we can be sure that the grace of God will always be in our souls. Through Jesus Christ our Lord. Amen.

THE LORD'S PRAYER

BLESSING

May the blessing of God the Father, God the Son and God the Holy Spirit, three persons and one God, come down on us and keep us always. Amen.

THE ROSARY

(During the month of October, the month of the Rosary, many will want to say a decade each day—that is quite sufficient for children. During the saying of the decade it is as well to give the children a few aids to thinking about the particular mystery, and it is suggested that the following readings be broken down to a few sentences which will be read before the start of the decade and a paragraph after about every three Hail Marys. This will help to keep thoughts fastened on to the mystery. The short meditation may also be useful for a particular feast of one of the mysteries. A suitable hymn may be sung and after the decade when the children have been trying to concentrate hard it is suggested that they be given a half-minute's silence either to dwell more on the thoughts that have been presented or simply to be silent and wait for the Holy Spirit to speak with them. An atmosphere of complete reverence is of course very necessary. More than ever in this kind of Assembly it is teacher and child praying together, not teacher imposing prayer on the child, and being concerned with the mechanics of 'taking prayers'.)

19. THE ANNUNCIATION

For a long time God's people had been waiting for a Saviour. At last, on a day chosen by our Heavenly Father, He sent the Angel Gabriel to a young Jewish girl called Mary, to ask if she would be the Mother of the Saviour He was to send. When Mary answered "Be it done to me according to your word", she brought the Son of God from heaven to earth. Her saying "Yes" to God gave each of us the chance to go to heaven.

Mary said "Yes" to God the Father. Her Son, Jesus Christ, God the Son, also showed us to say "Yes" to our Heavenly Father. When He knew He was going to be crucified, He said: "Not *my* will, but *thy* will be done."

It must be important for us to do our Father's will. We do His will when we think or say or do the things which please Him. Here is something for us to think about. We should often ask ourselves, "Are the things I am thinking about, or is what I am saying or what I am doing, pleasing to God? Jesus said, "I have come to do the will of my Father in heaven." This is to show us what we should do.

Our Lady's "Yes" to God the Father, and Jesus' "Yes" to His Father did wonderful things. God will never forget one time we say "Yes" to Him. "Be it done to me according to your word."

20. THE VISITATION

After Our Lady's great "Yes" when she had said to the Angel Gabriel, who brought her God's message, "Be it done unto me according to your word", she heard that her cousin Saint Elizabeth was also going to have a baby.

Our Lady was very pleased that she was going to have a baby and was very busy getting ready for the birth of Jesus. But she found time to go to visit Saint Elizabeth who lived about sixty miles away. It was a long and hard journey across the mountains, but she went because her cousin was old and perhaps needed her help.

Our Lady thought of others before herself and she went to tell Saint Elizabeth how pleased she was. We should always be pleased at the good things God gives to others and we should let them know how pleased we are for them.

Our Lady put herself out to visit her cousin. She did this to show us that we should do the same. She showed us that the best way of showing that we love God, whom we cannot see, is to love and help other people, and to pray for them, because Jesus came to our Blessed Lady and to all of us and shares His life and love with us.

As we finish this decade of the Rosary let us think of one way we can help our neighbour today for the love of God.

21. THE BIRTH OF OUR LORD

Just before our Lord was born an order was given that all people should go to their family city to have their names written down so that they could be counted. Our Lady and Saint Joseph had to go to Bethlehem from Nazareth. That was a long hard journey in winter time. They would rather have stayed at home. But they were obedient. They kept the rules of their country.

When they got to Bethlehem they could only find a poor stable, like a cave cut in the rock, to sleep in. Jesus was born in this stable. God had become man—a little baby who was to grow up and show us how to live as our Father in heaven wants us to live.

Jesus was poor. He was king of heaven and earth. He was not too proud to be born in a poor stable. He was poor and loved the poor. He said that although He was the Master of all, He had come to act like a servant and to help others. He told us that we should be like Him.

As we finish the Rosary we should think in the quiet of our own minds how we can be like Him. Can we do something for those who are not so well off as we are? We should thank God for sending His Son to us on the first Christmas day because if He had not come we would not have any chance of going to His heavenly kingdom. We would have had no Mass, no Baptism or Holy Communion. We would have had no share in the life and love of God.

22. THE PRESENTATION OF OUR LORD
IN THE TEMPLE

Very shortly after Jesus was born, Our Lady took Him to the Temple to make an offering of thanksgiving to God for the birth of her Son. This was the best gift that God could give to Our Lady. She did not forget to say "thank you". We should never forget to say thank you for all the good things God has given to us.

The holy man Simeon took Jesus in his arms. He knew that Jesus was the Saviour who had come to lead us back to our heavenly Father. He too thanked God for Jesus coming to save the world.

Jesus gave us His Holy Spirit in Baptism. We became the children of God. We had a share of His life and His love. Jesus comes to us in Holy Communion to give us all the strength we need to be good and kind and obedient and truthful. We need His help. Let us decide now to go to Holy Communion often so that Jesus can come to us. But never let us forget to thank Him for coming and for giving us the gift of Himself like Our Lady did.

23. THE FINDING IN THE TEMPLE

When Our Lady and Saint Joseph went to the Temple in Jerusalem, when Jesus was twelve years old, they took Jesus with them. When they set off home they thought that He was with their friends who were with them, but He was not. How sad they were when they could not find Him. How happy they were when they did find Him after three days. They found Him in the Temple with the teachers who were there.

Jesus had stayed behind in the Temple, which He said was His Father's house. "Why did you look for me?" He said. "Could you not tell that I must needs be in the place that belongs to my Father?" Jesus teaches us that He came to do the will of His Father. We should always try to do the things God wants us to do.

Jesus went back to Nazareth with Our Lady and Saint Joseph and He was obedient to them and grew up well-pleasing to God. He shows us by His example that one way of pleasing God is to be obedient to our parents and those over us. Let us try today to be obedient for Jesus' sake.

24. THE AGONY IN THE GARDEN

After the Last Supper, Jesus knew that He would soon be arrested and put to death. He went to pray to His Father. Jesus was a man as well as being God and He did not want to suffer and to die. He took Peter and James and John with Him to watch and pray. He knew that it was sin that made Him suffer. He teaches us that if ever we are in trouble or sad we should pray quietly to God our Father.

He did not want to suffer. He prayed that if it were possible God the Father would not let Him suffer. But He finished His prayer by saying, "Yet, not my will, but Thine be done." We should always be ready to do what God wants of us no matter how hard it is.

Jesus was quite ready to suffer and to die for us. He wanted to save us and to give us a chance to be with Him in heaven, because that was the Father's plan for Him. We should often ask God to show us what He wants of us. We should tell Him that we are ready to do what He wants. He will always help us. If we always do God's will He will raise us up and glorify us with Jesus in His heavenly Kingdom.

25. THE SCOURGING AT THE PILLAR

After His arrest, Jesus was tied to a pillar and whipped. He had done no wrong but He offered His sufferings for us. He did not grumble.

It was because people had so often turned away from God, had said "No" to God, and had pleased themselves, that they could do nothing which really pleased God. They were without His life and love. Jesus suffered to win back for us the friendship of God.

Jesus suffered this terrible scourging for us. He showed us that we should be ready to suffer for Him. We should be ready to be hurt rather than say "No" to God. Let us ask Him as we finish this decade, to let us be ready to suffer for Him if that is what He wants of us.

26. THE CROWNING WITH THORNS

Pilate had asked Jesus if He were a king. Jesus had said that He was a king but that His Kingdom was not of this world. The soldiers made fun of Him and made a crown of sharp thorns and pressed it on His head.

Jesus suffered all this for us. His kingdom of heaven is more important than anything on earth. It is worth suffering for. Anything that we have now will one day end. Sometimes we are happy. But not always. If we try to please Jesus, we shall one day be happy forever with Him in His kingdom.

We should try always to please Jesus, our king. He did not mind suffering for us or being made fun of. When we make our Morning Offering each morning when we get up we should remember that we offer Him the unpleasant things that happen to us. If anything makes us suffer or if anyone makes fun of us today for doing the things God wants of us we should think of Jesus our king. He suffered so much for us without grumbling.

27. JESUS CARRIES HIS CROSS TO CALVARY

Jesus was made to carry His cross on the rough road up Mount Calvary. It was heavy. His shoulders and back were already bruised and sore from His scourging. His head ached with the crown of thorns. Sometimes He was so weak that He fell under the heavy cross and was hurt more.

Jesus offered all this suffering to His heavenly Father for us.

Jesus loved us so much. We should love Him back. If we have to suffer unpleasant things we can tell Him that we will offer them up with Him because He did so much for us. We can offer them up to Him to try to make up for all the times we have decided to do the things we want, instead of what we know He wants us to do. Then, like Simon of Cyrene, we may perhaps, be helping our Lord to carry His cross.

28. JESUS DIES ON THE CROSS

Jesus was nailed to the Cross and was crucified. He was saying His great "Yes" to our heavenly Father. He was offering His life for us.

God our Father will forgive us all our sins if we are sorry for them because Jesus suffered and died for us. We should ask Jesus crucified to help us to be sorry for our sins and to try to make up for them.

We can only make up for them a little and have the life of God in us because Jesus has already offered Himself for us. Let us thank Him for His goodness to us and offer Him all that we think or say or do because He has been so good to us.

29. THE RESURRECTION OF OUR LORD

Jesus died but on the third day He rose again—He was alive again and could suffer and die no more. He was glorified. Because Jesus died and rose again, we will also rise again.

Sickness and suffering and death came into the world only because of sin. But at last, all these will end and we too will be glorified and will suffer no more. We will one day be with Jesus forever.

This could only happen because Jesus rose again. He did this so that we would have a chance to live as He really wants us to live. Let us tell Him that we will try to do this.

30. THE ASCENSION

For forty days, Jesus kept appearing to His Apostles. He told them that He was going back to heaven, to His Father, so that He could prepare a place for us.

Jesus has a place for us in His heavenly kingdom. He wants us with Him. To be sure of being with Him we must love God and all our neighbours. We must try to live just as we think that Jesus wants us to live. He teaches us how to love. He gives us His life and His love in the Sacrament of Baptism, in Holy Communion and the other Sacraments. He gives us the Church, the priests, our parents and teachers to help us.

Jesus, I long to be with you in your kingdom. Help me never to do anything which will keep me away from you. I need your help. I will try to do the things you want me to do.

31. THE COMING OF THE HOLY SPIRIT

Before Jesus went back to His Father, He promised that He would send His Holy Spirit to His Church to be with us always. Before the Holy Spirit came the Apostles were afraid. They knew that they were weak and could do nothing on their own.

When the Holy Spirit came the Apostles knew that they could do all that Jesus wanted. They became strong and were frightened no more. They did everything to help people to love God.

Jesus sent His Holy Spirit to us when we were Baptised. When we grew up a little He sent Him again to strengthen us in the Sacrament of Confirmation. Jesus has given us His Holy Spirit so that we have every help we need. Let us listen to what the Spirit of Jesus wants of us. In the quiet of our own minds let us thank Jesus for His Holy Spirit and ask Him what He wants us to do today.

32. OUR LADY IS TAKEN UP TO HEAVEN

Our Lady was God's most perfect creature because she never at any time turned away from God. She loved God more and more every day of her life. When she died, because she had never at any time said "No" to God, He took her body and soul up to heaven to be with Him for ever.

This is what God intended for us all. But sin stopped this. Jesus died and rose again to give us a chance at last to be with Him. When He comes in glory our bodies too, will rise again to be with Him for ever.

Mary's body is already glorified and in heaven because she never sinned. Her body was taken up to heaven because of this and to show us that our bodies too will be glorified. Then God's kingdom will have come.

33. OUR LADY IS CROWNED AS QUEEN OF HEAVEN

Our Lady was the mother of Jesus and was taken to heaven body and soul when she died. She is glorified and because she is the most perfect and pleasing of God's creatures she was crowned as Queen of Heaven.

Our Lady is Queen of the Angels and Saints and she is our queen too. She is queen of all God's kingdom. She wants us to be with Jesus in His kingdom. She is praying for us and is always ready to help us.

We should never let a day pass without remembering that Our Lady is Queen of Heaven and is waiting for us, to take us to her Son. She is our mother and will never refuse us anything which will help us to praise and love God. How happy we should be at our Lady's happiness and glory now that she is Queen of Heaven. Our Lady, Queen of Heaven, pray for us that, one day, we may be glorified with you.

34. FEAST OF THE GUARDIAN ANGELS

V. I have lifted up my eyes to the hills.
R. From whence my help shall come.
V. My help comes from the Lord.
R. Who made heaven and earth.

HYMN

READING

Listen today to the Good News told by Saint Matthew.

At that time the disciples came to Jesus, saying, "Who is the greatest in the kingdom of heaven?" And calling to him a child, he put him in the midst of them, and said, "Truly, I say to you, unless you turn and become like children, you will never enter the kingdom of heaven. Whoever humbles himself like this child, he is the greatest in the kingdom of heaven.

"Whoever receives one such child in my name receives me.

"See that you do not despise one of these little ones; for I tell you that in heaven their angels always behold the face of my Father who is in heaven."

PRAYER

O God, you have been so good as to send your holy angels to watch over us. Please hear us when we ask that we may always be safe under their protection. May we be happy in their company with you through all eternity. Through our Lord Jesus Christ your Son, who lives and reigns with you, in the unity of the Holy Spirit, for ever and ever. Amen.

THE LORD'S PRAYER

BLESSING

May God bless us and all those we shall see or speak with today. Amen.

c

35. SAINT THERESA OF LISEEUX

V. O Lord open my lips!

R. And my mouth will declare your praise.
   Glory be to the Father. . . .

HYMN

READING

Saint Theresa was quite an ordinary little girl who became a very great saint. She lived in France and was very happy at home with her mother and father and her sisters. She played and she went to church and was always very cheerful even though she was not very strong.

She loved God very much and wanted to do great things for Him. She had heard about the martyrs who had given their lives for God. She had heard of brave men and women who went to the Mission countries where there were so many people who did not know and love God. She knew that she would not be strong enough to go to the Missions. She was only young and not a very important person and she knew that she could not do any of the great and brave things that so many saints had done. She was very like us.

Like us she knew that God wanted her to be a saint. She prayed that God would show her what to do. He wanted her to be a nun in a Carmelite convent. She became a nun when she was about fifteen. She learned the prayers which the nuns said and how to do her work and to live her life as a nun.

How did she become a saint? She knew that she would never be able to do any really great things, so she said to herself, "I know what I will do. I will do all the ordinary, little things that I am supposed to do as well as I possibly can all the time". That was how she became a great saint. She was not a martyr but when she was sick she offered her illness to God. She never went to the missions but her prayers helped many missionaries to teach many people to learn to know and to love God.

This is the way in which God wants most of us to be saints—just by doing all the things that we know we should do as well as we possibly can. If we really try to do the things we offer to God in our Morning Offering we too shall be very close to God and very pleasing to Him.

PRAYER

Dear Jesus, please help us to be like Saint Theresa, and to do all the things we know you want us to do as well as we possibly can. By your help we know that we shall be able to be pleasing to you and to join you at last with Saint Theresa in your Heavenly kingdom, for ever and ever. Amen.

THE LORD'S PRAYER

BLESSING

May the blessing of God, the Father, the Son and the Holy Spirit come down on us and be with us always. Amen.

36. THE HOLY SOULS

V. Our help is in the name of the Lord.
R. Who made heaven and earth.
   I confess to Almighty God. . . .

HYMN

READING

During our time on earth we should be getting ready to go to God's heavenly kingdom. God made us to know him, to love him and to serve him in this life so that we shall be ready to share the joys of heaven with him.

But we have all offended God our Father by our sins. We do not deserve to live with Him. If, when we die we are not quite ready to go to heaven because of our sins, then we must suffer for them in Purgatory.

The souls in Purgatory will certainly one day see God. But for a while they must be punished. The souls in Purgatory cannot help themselves. We can help them. The best way of all to help them is to offer the Holy Mass for them. We can help them too by our other prayers and little acts of penance. We can help them to be with God more quickly.

We should pray especially for our dead relations and friends. There are those in Purgatory who have no friends on earth to pray for them. We should often remember the forgotten souls in Purgatory.

The month of November is the month when we specially remember the souls in Purgatory. We should decide today to do something each day of the month for the Holy Souls.

PRAYER

O God, the Creator and Redeemer of all the faithful, grant to the souls of the faithful departed, remission of their sins. May our prayers help them to be with you in your Heavenly kingdom, who livest and reignest world without end. Amen.

THE LORD'S PRAYER

BLESSING

Eternal rest give to them O Lord and may perpetual light shine upon them. May they rest in peace. Amen.

37. THE HOLY SOULS

V. I have lifted up my eyes to the hills.
R. From whence my help comes.
V. My help comes from the Lord.
R. Who made heaven and earth.
   Glory be to the Father. . . .

HYMN

READING

The reading today tells how the Jewish people were to help those who had died.

And the noble Judas exhorted the people to keep themselves free from sin. In doing this he acted very well and honourably, taking account of the resurrection. For if he were not expecting that those who had fallen would rise again, it would have been foolish to pray for the dead. But if he was looking to the splendid reward that is laid up for those who fall asleep in godliness, it was a holy and pious thought. Therefore he made atonement for the dead, that they might be delivered from their sin.

PRAYER

Lord have mercy on the Holy Souls. They cannot help themselves. Listen to our prayers for them and grant that our prayers and penances may help them quickly to enjoy never ending happiness with you in your heavenly kingdom. We ask this through Jesus Christ Your Son, our Lord, who lives and reigns with you, in the unity of the Holy Spirit, world without end. Amen.

THE LORD'S PRAYER

BLESSING

May the most high, the most just, the most adorable Will of God be done, praised and exalted in all things for evermore. Amen.

38. THE MISSIONS

V. Our Lady, Queen of Apostles.
R. Pray for us.
V. Queen of the Missions.
R. Pray for us.

HYMN

READING

This morning's reading tells us how our Lord sent his apostles to preach to the people. Saint Luke tells the story.

After this the Lord appointed seventy others, and sent them on ahead of him, two by two, into every town and place where he himself was about to come. And he said to them, "The harvest is plentiful, but the labourers are few; pray therefore the Lord of the harvest to send out labourers into his harvest. Go your way; behold, I send you out as lambs in the midst of wolves. Carry no purse, no bag, no sandals; and salute no one on the road. Whatever house you enter, first say, 'Peace be to this house!' And if a son of peace is there, your peace shall rest upon him; but if not, it shall return to you. And remain in the same house, eating and drinking what they provide, for the labourer deserves his wages; do not go from house to house. Whenever you enter a town and they receive you, eat what is set before you; heal the sick in it and say to them, 'The kingdom of God has come near to you.'

"He who hears you hears me, and he who rejects you rejects me, and he who rejects me rejects him who sent me."

PRAYER

O God who wills that all men should be saved and come to the knowledge of truth: send out, we pray you, labourers into your vineyard and help them to speak your word with confidence so that all people may know you the one true God and Jesus Christ your Son who lives and reigns with you and the Holy Spirit, world without end. Amen.

THE LORD'S PRAYER

BLESSING

Lord hear our prayer and bless all those who work in foreign lands for the glory of your name. Amen.

39. THE GRAIN OF MUSTARD SEED

V. O Lord, open my lips!
R. And my mouth will declare your praise.
   Glory be to the Father. . . .

HYMN

READING

Today we hear the story our Lord told of the very small seed which can grow into a large plant. He told it to show us how, if we look after the graces which God gives us, they will grow and make us more pleasing to God. The story is from the Gospel according to Saint Mark.

And he said, "With what can we compare the kingdom of God, or what parable shall we use for it? It is like a grain of mustard seed, which, when sown upon the ground, is the smallest of all the seeds on earth; yet when it is sown it grows up and becomes the greatest of all shrubs, and puts forth large branches, so that the birds of the air can make nests in its shade."

41

PRAYER

O God, you have put the word of your life and your love in our hearts, by our Baptism. Help us to keep it strong within us. May we always serve you cheerfully, doing all things for love of you so that we may bless and glorify you in all that we do, through Jesus Christ our Lord. Amen.

THE LORD'S PRAYER

BLESSING

May the peace of God, which passes all understanding, keep our minds and hearts in the knowledge and love of Christ Jesus our Lord. Amen.

40. THE LILIES OF THE FIELD

V. Blessed be the Holy and Undivided Trinity!
R. Now and for evermore. Amen.

HYMN

READING

The reading today tells us of how God our Father looks after all of his creation, but especially after us. It is taken from the Good News told by Saint Matthew.

"Therefore I tell you, do not be anxious about your life, what you shall eat or what you shall drink, nor about your body, what you shall put on. Is not life more than food, and the body more than clothing? Look at the birds of the air; they neither sow nor reap nor gather into barns, and yet your heavenly Father feeds them. Are you not of more value than they? And which of you by being anxious can add one cubit to his span of life? And why are you anxious about clothing? Consider the lilies of the field, how they grow; they neither toil nor spin; yet I tell you, even Solomon in all his glory was not arrayed like one of these. But if God so clothes the grass of the field, which today is alive and tomorrow is thrown into the oven, will He not much more clothe you, O men of little faith? Therefore do not be anxious, saying, 'What shall we eat?' or 'What shall we drink?' or 'What shall we wear?' For the Gentiles seek all these things; and your heavenly Father knows that you need them all. But seek first His kingdom and His righteousness, and all these things shall be yours as well.

"Therefore do not be anxious about tomorrow, for tomorrow will be anxious for itself. Let the day's own trouble be sufficient for the day."

PRAYER

Show us clearly, O God, what you want us to do today. Help us to do our best both in school and at home. And having done our best may we confidently leave the rest to you. Through our Lord and Saviour Jesus Christ who lives and reigns with you, in the unity of the Holy Spirit, world without end. Amen.

THE LORD'S PRAYER

BLESSING

Give to us O God, a quiet mind, free from care and worry, that we may cheerfully continue our journey to your heavenly kingdom; through Jesus Christ our Lord. Amen.

41. HONOUR ALL MEN

V. Show us Lord your mercy.

R. And grant us your salvation.

V. O Lord, hear my prayer!

R. And let my cry come to you!

I confess to almighty God. . . .

HYMN

READING

Saint Peter tells us today in his first Epistle how we should behave towards various people and how we can try to become saints.

Be subject for the Lord's sake to every human institution, whether it be to the king, or to governors as sent by him to punish those who do wrong and to praise those who do right. For it is God's will that by doing right you should put to silence the ignorance of foolish men. Live as free men, yet without using your freedom as a pretext for evil; but live as servants of God. Honour all men. Love the brotherhood. Fear God. Honour the king.

For

"He that would love life
and see good days,
let him keep his tongue from evil
and his lips from speaking guile;
let him turn away from evil and do right;
let him seek peace and pursue it.
For the eyes of the Lord are upon the righteous,
and his ears are open to their prayer."

PRAYER

Dear Jesus, help us to be obedient, truthful and honest and always to try to do the things which please you. Keep us and our friends from all danger. Forgive us our sins and bring us at last to your kingdom, where we may give endless praise to God our Father, for ever and ever. Amen.

THE LORD'S PRAYER

BLESSING

May God the Father, God the Son and God the Holy Spirit, bless us and keep us now and for evermore. Amen.

42. BELONGING TO GOD

V. We adore you, O Christ and we praise you!

R. Because by your holy Cross you have redeemed the world.

HYMN

READING

When God called Abraham to leave his country and told him to journey to a strange land, Abraham did exactly what God told him. He was just getting to know God but he had faith in God's promises. He did not really understand all that God wanted of him but he obeyed. This was real faith and because Abraham answered God's call in obedience and trust God rewarded him. Abraham was rewarded because he gave himself completely to God, to do all that God wanted him to do.

Abraham lived long before our Lord. He had very few helps to show him what pleased God but he gave himself to God completely because God had made him a promise.

We have so much more chance to know God because Our Lord has come and taught us many things and left us many helps to keep us close to God. He has given us a share of His life and love through our baptism. If we offend God, we can become His friends again and receive extra help by the Sacrament of Penance. Most of all he has left us Himself in Holy Communion. He has promised us a share of His kingdom.

But do we really belong to God? Have we really given ourselves to Him to do all that He wants of us? To do only what He wants of us?

Let us tell God our Father today that we will try to have faith like Abraham's and that we will try to belong to Him completely. Let us tell Him that if we know what He wants of us we will do it, even though we do not properly understand. He has done so much for us and has promised us a share in His kingdom if we do things in His name.

PRAYER

O Lord, you have taught us that the worst that can happen to us is to lose our faith in you. Give us always a strong faith which will ever keep us in your love so that at last we may join with Our Lady and all the saints in praising you forever in your kingdom. Grant this dear Father in Heaven for the sake of your Son Jesus Christ our Lord. Amen.

THE LORD'S PRAYER

BLESSING

May God Our Father bless us with His Holy Spirit and keep us strong in faith, through Jesus Christ our Lord. Amen.

43. SAINT MARTIN OF TOURS

V. O Lord, open my lips!
R. And my mouth will declare your praise!
   Glory be to the Father. . . .

HYMN

READING

Saint Martin of Tours was a soldier in the Roman army. He lived about one thousand six hundred years ago. One of the most famous stories about him was of the time when he was learning about the Catholic faith and before he received the life and love of God by Baptism.

One night, Martin met a beggar who was very cold, and whose clothes were all torn and ragged. Saint Martin, an officer in the army, was wrapped up in a large warm cloak. He felt sorry for the beggar. To be sorry

46

for someone means that we will do something for them. To be sorry is not to feel something but to do something. Saint Martin cut his cloak in half with his sword and gave one half to the beggar who now had plenty to keep him warm.

At once our Lord showed Martin that this kind deed had been done to himself. Our Lord tells us "If you give so much as a cup of cold water in my name, you give it to me".

We should try to follow the example of Saint Martin in having a great love for the poor. Most of us have never known what it is like to be really hungry and cold and to have no home at all. There are many people in many parts of the world who need our help. There are people in our own parish who are worse off than we are. Try to do something to help them. Perhaps several groups could get together sometime later today to talk about helping. When you have decided what you can do, do it. Your teachers will help you if you need their help. Remember that we are not sorry for the poor and the needy unless we do something for them. Pray to Saint Martin to show you how to help them.

Later Saint Martin was baptised. He became a priest, a missioner and a great Bishop of Tours in France.

PRAYER

May the example of Saint Martin help us to think more kindly of the poor and suffering. There are many people who are cold and have not enough blankets for their beds, no heating in their homes and not enough food to keep them healthy. Dear Jesus, help us often to remember them in our prayers and to help them with gifts whenever we can, for your sake. Amen.

THE LORD'S PRAYER

BLESSING

From forgetfulness of His great love and of His poor may the Lord deliver us. May He teach us to walk humbly in His ways, now and always. Amen.

44. ADVICE TO TIMOTHY

V. I have lifted up my eyes to the hills.
R. From whence my help comes.

V. My help comes from the Lord.
R. Who made heaven and earth.
Glory be to the Father. . . .

HYMN

READING

Saint Paul reminds Timothy of some of the things which keep us from the love of God and gives him some good advice on how to keep close to God. The reading is from his first letter to Timothy.

For we brought nothing into the world, and we cannot take anything out of the world; but if we have food and clothing, with these we shall be content. But those who desire to be rich fall into temptation, into a snare, into many senseless and hurtful desires that plunge men into ruin and destruction. For the love of money is the root of all evils; it is through this craving that some have wandered away from the faith and pierced their hearts with many pangs.

But as for you, man of God, shun all this; aim at virtue, have Christ as your example. Have a strong faith and love God and your neighbour. Be gentle. Fight the good fight of the faith; take hold of the eternal life to which you were called when you made the good confession in the presence of many witnesses.

PRAYER

O Lord, the Saviour of sinners and our help in every time of need, hear our prayers and help us to hear your word with understanding so that we may follow its teachings always until we reach your everlasting kingdom. We ask this for the sake of Jesus Christ your Son, who lives and reigns with you, in the unity of the Holy Spirit, world without end. Amen.

THE LORD'S PRAYER

BLESSING

Teach us, good Lord, to serve you as you deserve;
to give and not to count the cost;
to fight and not to heed the wounds;
to toil and not to seek for rest;
to labour for you and not to ask for any reward,
save that of knowing that we are doing your will.
Through Jesus Christ our Lord. Amen.

45. GREETINGS FROM SAINT PAUL

V. Our help is in the name of the Lord!
R. Who made heaven and earth!
I confess to almighty God. . . .

HYMN

READING

Today we are going to hear some very lovely words from Saint Paul's letter to the Philippians.

Rejoice in the Lord always; again I will say, Rejoice. The Lord is at hand. Have no anxiety about anything, but in everything by prayer and supplication with thanksgiving let your requests be made known to God. And the peace of God, which passes all understanding, will keep your hearts and your minds in Christ Jesus.
Finally, brethren, whatever is true, whatever is honourable, whatever is just, whatever is pure, whatever is lovely, whatever is gracious, if there is any excellence, if there is anything worthy of praise, think about these things.

PRAYER

Fill our minds and our hearts with thoughts that are good and pure so that we may find no place for that which is displeasing to you, O Lord. And as you place in our minds good desires, give us the help to do them, by living the kind of life which is well pleasing to you. We ask this for the sake of Jesus Christ our Lord. Amen.

THE LORD'S PRAYER

BLESSING

May the blessing of God Almighty, the Father, the Son and God the Holy Spirit, be amongst us and remain with us always. Amen.

46. DO NOT BE ANGRY

V. Show us Lord, your mercy!
R. And grant us your salvation.
V. Lord, hear my prayer!
R. And let my cry come to you.

HYMN

READING

The reading today is from Saint Paul's letter to the people who lived at Ephesus and who had not long been Christians. What he says to them is for us too for it is the Word of God.

Therefore, putting away falsehood, let every one speak the truth with his neighbour, for we are members one of another. Do not let the sun go down on your anger, and give no opportunity to the devil. Let the thief no longer steal, but rather let him labour, doing honest work with his hands, so that he may be able to give to those in need. Let no evil talk come out of your mouths, but only such as is good for edifying, as fits the occasion, that it may impart grace to those who hear. And do not grieve the Holy Spirit of God, in whom you were sealed for the day of redemption. Let all bitterness, and wrath, and anger, and clamour, and lies, or lies about your neighbours, be put away from you. Be kind to one another, tenderhearted, forgiving one another, as God in Christ forgave you.

PRAYER

Dear Lord, we are often angry with our friends. Help us to show them more kindness and to be more forgiving like Jesus is. We are sorry for our faults. Please forgive us and do not remember our sins but our efforts to do what is right and pleasing to you. We ask it for your Name's sake. Amen.

THE LORD'S PRAYER

BLESSING

May we go forward with the light of hope in our eyes, your word on our lips, and your love in our heart, now and always. Amen.

47. BE STRONG IN THE LORD

V. Come, Holy Spirit, fill the hearts of your faithful, and kindle in them the fire of your love!
R. Send forth your Spirit and they shall be created,
And you will renew the face of the earth!

HYMN

READING

Today's reading is again from Saint Paul's letter to the Ephesians.

Finally, be strong in the Lord and in the strength of His might. Put on the whole armour of God, that you may be able to stand against the wiles of the devil. Therefore take the whole armour of God, that you may be able to withstand in the evil day, and having done all, to stand. Stand therefore, having girded your loins with truth, and having put on the breastplate of righteousness, and having shod your feet with the equipment of the gospel of peace; above all taking the shield of faith, with which you can quench all the flaming darts of the evil one. And take the helmet of salvation, and the sword of the Spirit, which is the word of God. Pray at all times in the Spirit, for all Christians.

PRAYER

Lord, we need your help all the time. We can do nothing unless you help us. Protect and guard us against all temptations for the sake of Jesus Christ your Son our Lord. Amen.

THE LORD'S PRAYER

BLESSING

May the peace of God which passes all understanding, keep our hearts and minds in the knowledge and the love of God and of His Son, Jesus Christ our Lord. And may the blessing of God, the Father, the Son and the Holy Spirit, be with us always. Amen.

48. THE DEN OF LIONS

V. Our help is in the name of the Lord!
R. Who made heaven and earth!
    I confess to Almighty God. . . .

HYMN

READING

Once when the Jewish people were taken off to a foreign country they were told to pray to false gods and to do things which would not please God. Daniel, a young man, refused to do this. His good example helped his people to stay true to God in times of great difficulty. We read the story in the Book of Daniel.

Then the king commanded, and Daniel was brought and cast into the den of lions. The king said to Daniel, "May your God, whom you serve continually, deliver you!" And a stone was brought and laid upon the mouth of the den, and the king sealed it with his own signet and with the signet of his lords, that nothing might be changed concerning Daniel. Then the king went to his palace, and spent the night fasting; no diversions were brought to him, and sleep fled from him. Then, at break of day, the king arose and went in haste to the den of lions. When he came near to the den where Daniel was, he cried out in a tone of anguish and said to Daniel, "O Daniel, servant of the living God, has your God, whom you serve continually, been able to deliver you from the lions?" Then Daniel said to the king, "O king, live for ever! My God sent his angel and shut the lions' mouths, and they have not hurt me, because I was found blameless before him; and also before you, O king, I have done no wrong." Then the king was exceedingly glad, and commanded that Daniel be taken up out of the den. So Daniel was taken up out of the den, and no kind of hurt was found upon him, because he had trusted in his God.

PRAYER

Lord help us always to do what we know you want us to do, even though others may be doing what is wrong. Make us strong to be good examples to those who do not know and love you so that with your help we may be able to bring them to you. Do not let us be afraid to do what you want. Give us the trust in you that Daniel had. We ask this for the sake of Jesus your Son and our Saviour. Amen.

THE LORD'S PRAYER

BLESSING

Defend us, your children, with your grace, O Lord, that we may be yours for ever. Send us your Holy Spirit so that we may come at last to your heavenly kingdom, through Jesus Christ our Lord. Amen.

53

49. THANKS BE TO GOD

V. I have lifted up my eyes to the hills!

R. From whence my help comes.

V. My help comes from the Lord.

R. Who made heaven and earth!

Glory be to the Father. . . .

HYMN

READING

Today we are going to give thanks to God for the promise of the Resurrection when we shall all be joined again to our glorified bodies and shall be with our risen Lord in His heavenly Kingdom.

This is the greatest thing we can pray for and thank God for.

No matter how poor we are, or how sick or sad or worried we are, no matter how hard everything may seem, we know that if we do what our Heavenly Father wants of us, He will take us at last to Himself, to be with Him forever.

Our Lord was poor; He suffered, people laughed at Him and treated Him badly but He kept on doing what His Heavenly Father wanted. And our Lord rose again after He had been cruelly put to death and His glorified Body is now with His Heavenly Father to prepare a place for us.

If our Lord had not suffered and risen again we would have had no chance to be with His Father forever in His kingdom.

Let us then pray with Saint Paul, "Thanks be to God who has given us victory through our Lord Jesus Christ."

PRAYER

We thank you Lord, because you have promised that whoever lives his life here on earth doing your will shall have life everlasting with you in your heavenly kingdom. Send us your Holy Spirit to put good thoughts into our minds, and the help to do your will, so that we shall be taken to the glory of your kingdom, through Jesus Christ our Lord. Amen.

THE LORD'S PRAYER

BLESSING

O God, save us waking and guard us sleeping, that awake we may watch with Christ and asleep we may rest in peace, through Jesus Christ our Lord. Amen.

50. PRAISE AND TRUST IN GOD

V. We adore you, O Christ, and we praise you!
R. Because by your holy Cross you have redeemed the world!

HYMN

READING

Psalm 146 which we are going to read is a wonderful song of praise. I will stop after each verse so that you can all call out *"Praise the Lord"*. Be ready to join in;

Praise the Lord!
Praise the Lord, O my soul! —
I will praise the Lord as long as I live; —
 I will sing praises to my God while I have being. —
I will praise the Lord,
who made heaven and earth, the sea, and all that is
 in them; —
who keeps faith for ever; —
who looks after those in trouble; —
who gives food to the hungry. —
The Lord sets the prisoners free; —
 the Lord opens the eyes of the blind. —
The Lord lifts up those who are bowed down; —
 the Lord loves the righteous. —
The Lord upholds the widow and the fatherless; —
 but the way of the wicked he brings to ruin. —
Praise the Lord!

PRAYER

We praise you Lord for your goodness, your holiness and your truth. We trust that you will give us every help we need to follow your example faithfully as your Son Jesus Christ our Lord showed us. Amen.

THE LORD'S PRAYER

BLESSING

May the peace of God which passes all understanding, keep our hearts and minds in the knowledge and love of Christ Jesus our Lord. Amen.

51. ASKING AND RECEIVING

V. Our help is in the name of the Lord!
R. Who made heaven and earth!
    I confess to Almighty God. . . .

HYMN

READING

Our parents are very good to us but no matter how good they are we know that our heavenly Father knows how to help us even more. Our Lord Himself tells us this in the Gospel according to Saint Matthew.

"Ask, and it will be given you; seek, and you will find; knock, and it will be opened to you. For every one who asks receives, and he who seeks finds, and to him who knocks it will be opened. Or what man of you, if his son asks him for bread, will give him a stone? Or if he asks for a fish, will give him a serpent? If you then, who are evil, know how to give good gifts to your children, how much more will your Father who is in heaven give good things to those who ask him! So whatever you wish that men would do to you, do so to them for this is the law and the prophets."

PRAYER

Dear Jesus, you said, "Ask and you shall receive". Teach us to ask for the things that we need to help us to be pleasing to you. All the good things we have are given by you. We thank you for all your great gifts to us. We do not deserve your great goodness. Help us to be truly good and pleasing to you so that we may at last be with you and the Father and the Holy Spirit for ever and ever. Amen.

THE LORD'S PRAYER

BLESSING

May the Lord bless us and keep us and may his light shine on us and give us his peace, for ever more. Amen.

52. THE CENTURION'S FAITH

V. O Lord, open my lips!
R. And my mouth will declare your praise.
Glory be to the Father. . . .

HYMN

READING

A Roman Officer who was in Israel at the time of our Lord shows his strong faith in the power of Jesus. He was one of the first who was not a Jew to believe. Jesus wants us all to have a great faith and trust in Him and to show our love for Him. Listen to the story of the Centurion from Saint Luke's Good News.

After he had ended all his sayings in the hearing of the people he entered Capernaum. Now a centurion had a slave who was dear to him, who was sick and at the point of death. When he heard of Jesus, he sent to him elders of the Jews, asking Him to come and heal his slave. And when they came to Jesus, they besought him earnestly, saying, "He is worthy to have you do this for him, for he loves our nation, and he built us our synagogue. And Jesus went with them. When he was not far from the house, the centurion sent friends to him, saying to him, "Lord, do not trouble yourself, for I am not worthy to have you come under my roof; therefore I did not presume to come to you. But say the word, and let my servant be healed. For I am a man set under authority, with soldiers under me: and I say to one, 'Go', and he goes; and to another, 'Come', and he comes; and to my slave, 'Do this', and he does it." When Jesus heard this he marvelled at him, and turned and said to the multitude that followed him, "I tell you, not even in Israel have I found such faith." And when those who had been sent returned to the house, they found the slave well.

PRAYER

My God I believe in you and all your church teaches, because you have said it and your Word is true.

THE LORD'S PRAYER

BLESSING

May the blessing of God the Father, God the Son and God the Holy Spirit, be with us now and always.

53. THE HOUSE BUILT ON A ROCK

V. Show us Lord your mercy!
R. And grant us your salvation.
V. Lord, hear my prayer!
R. And let my cry come to you.
   Glory be to the Father. . . .

HYMN

READING

Yesterday we heard of the great faith of the Centurion. Today Saint Matthew tells us how Our Lord said that our faith must be very strong.

"Every one then who hears these words of mine and does them will be like a wise man who built his house upon the rock; and the rain fell, and the floods came, and the winds blew and beat upon that house, but it did not fall, because it had been founded on the rock. And every one who hears these words of mine and does not do them will be like a foolish man who built his house upon the sand; and the rain fell, and the floods came, and the winds blew and beat against that house, and it fell; and great was the fall of it."

PRAYER

Grant that our faith may be strong and safe against all temptations, O Lord. We know that it will be if only we will listen to your word in the Holy Bible and to the teachings of your church. We ask this in the name of Jesus Christ your Son who lives and reigns with you in the unity of the same Holy Spirit, world without end. Amen.

THE LORD'S PRAYER

BLESSING

May the Lord bless us and keep us and may the Lord make His Face to shine on us and to give us His peace, now and for evermore. Amen.

54. THE CENTURION'S SERVANT

V. Blessed be the Holy and Undivided Trinity!
R. Now and forever more! Amen.

HYMN

READING

Saint Matthew tells us of the faith of the Centurion. We heard this story the other day. See if you can see

59

another message in it. We know how important faith is. Without it we cannot be members of God's heavenly kingdom. We should thank God for this great gift and say with the centurion, "Lord, I am not worthy!" Listen now to the words of the Gospel:

As he entered Capernaum, a centurion came forward to him, beseeching him and saying, "Lord, my servant is lying paralyzed at home, in terrible distress." And he said to him, "I will come and heal him." But the centurion answered him, "Lord, I am not worthy to have you come under my roof; but only say the word, and my servant will be healed. For I am a man under authority, with soldiers under me; and I say to one, 'Go', and he goes, and to another, 'Come', and he comes, and to my slave, 'Do this', and he does it." When Jesus heard him he marvelled, and said to those who followed him, "Truly, I say to you, not even in Israel have I found such faith. I tell you, many will come from east and west and sit at table with Abraham, Isaac, and Jacob in the kingdom of heaven, while the sons of the kingdom will be thrown into the outer darkness; there men will weep and gnash their teeth." And to the centurion Jesus said, "Go; be it done for you as you have believed." And the servant was healed at that very moment.

PRAYER

Lord, increase my faith,
fix all my hopes on you,
and give me a great love of you and your Holy church,
through Jesus Christ our Lord. Amen.

THE LORD'S PRAYER

BLESSING

Save us O Lord waking and guard us sleeping, that awake we may watch with Christ and asleep we may rest in peace. Amen.

55. THE CRIPPLE AT THE POOL

V. O God, come to my assistance!
R. O Lord make haste to help me!
   Glory be to the Father. . . .

HYMN

READING

Today's reading comes from the Good News told by Saint John. In this reading you will see how our Lord rewarded the great patience of the poor cripple who had nobody to help him. But he trusted in the power of Our Lord.

Now there is in Jerusalem by the Sheep Gate a pool, in Hebrew called Bethzatha, which has five porticoes. In these lay a multitude of invalids, blind, lame, paralyzed. One man was there, who had been ill for thirty-eight years. When Jesus saw him and knew that he had been lying there a long time, he said to him, "Do you want to be healed?" The sick man answered him, "Sir, I have no man to put me into the pool when the water is troubled, and while I am going another steps down before me." Jesus said to him, "Rise, take up your pallet, and walk." And at once the man was healed, and he took up his pallet and walked.

PRAYER

Dear Jesus, give us the gift of patiently waiting for those things we ask for and the grace to ask only for those things which are pleasing to you. Help us to do your will in all things and to serve you all the days of our lives. Amen.

THE LORD'S PRAYER

BLESSING

May the Lord forgive what we have been, make holy what we are and order what shall be for the sake of Jesus Christ our Lord. Amen.

56. "HAPPY IS THE MAN WHO FINDS WISDOM"

V. O Lord, open my lips!
R. And my mouth shall declare your praise!
   Glory be to the Father. . . .

HYMN

READING

To be truly wise is to know and love and serve God. This is the meaning of today's reading from the Book of Proverbs.

> Happy is the man who finds wisdom,
>   and the man who gets understanding,
> for the gain from it is better than gain from silver
>   and its profit better than gold.
> She is more precious than jewels,
>   and nothing you desire can compare with her.
> Long life is in her right hand;
>   in her left hand are riches and honour.
> Her ways are ways of pleasantness,
>   and all her paths are peace.

PRAYER

As we grow up in this school, O Lord, help us not only to get better at our lessons but to get to know and love you more and more. Then when we have left school grant that we may continue to love and serve you. Grant that our lives may lead in the end to your everlasting kingdom of heaven. Grant this, O God, for the sake of Jesus Christ our Lord. Amen.

THE LORD'S PRAYER

BLESSING

The grace of our Lord Jesus Christ, and the love of God and the fellowship of the Holy Spirit, be with us all evermore. Amen.

57. DOERS OF THE WORD

V. Show us Lord your mercy!
R. And grant us your salvation.
V. Lord, hear my prayer!
R. And let my cry come to you!
   Glory be to the Father. . . .

HYMN

READING

It is not enough to know what God wants of us. We have to do what He wants of us if we are to please Him. Saint James tells us this in his first epistle. He tells us that the best way to keep God's law is to help our neighbour.

But be doers of the word, and not hearers only, deceiving yourselves. For if any one is a hearer of the word and not a doer, he is like a man who observes his natural face in a mirror; for he observes himself and goes away and at once forgets what he was like. If any one thinks he is religious, and does not bridle his tongue but deceives his heart, this man's religion is vain. Religion that is pure and undefiled before God and the Father is this: to visit orphans and widows in their affliction, and to keep oneself unstained from the world.

PRAYER

Dear Lord! Help us to spend ourselves for the poor and for all those who are in any sort of trouble. In this way we shall show you that we really love you. We ask this for the sake of Jesus Christ our Lord. Amen.

THE LORD'S PRAYER

BLESSING

May God be merciful to us and bless us. May he give us the grace to know what He wants of us and the help we need to do it. Amen.

58. "GOD IS LOVE"

V. Blessed be the Holy and Undivided Trinity!
R. Now and for evermore. Amen.

HYMN

READING

Listen to these beautiful words from the first epistle of Saint John.

Beloved, let us love one another; for love is of God, and he who loves is born of God and knows God. He who does not love does not know God; for God is love. In this the love of God was made manifest among us, that God sent His only Son into the world, so that we might live through Him. In this is love, not that we loved God but that He loved us and sent His Son to be the expiation for our sins. Beloved, if God so loved us, we also ought to love one another. No man has ever seen God; if we love one another, God abides in us and His love is perfected in us. If any one says, "I love God," and hates his brother, he is a liar; for he who does not love his brother whom he has seen, cannot love God whom he has not seen. And this commandment we have from Him, that he who loves God should love his brother also.

PRAYER

O God, help us to show brotherly love to all those we meet, whether they are friendly or not. Do not let us be disappointed if our efforts do not seem to make others more friendly to us. We know that your ways are not our ways. Let it be enough for us to know that we are doing what you want of us. We ask this through Jesus Christ your Son who loved us so very much. Amen.

THE LORD'S PRAYER

BLESSING

To you, O God, be all might, majesty, dominion and praise, now and for evermore. Amen.

59. PATIENCE AND LOVE

V. I have lifted up my eyes to the hills!
R. From whence my help comes.
V. My help comes from the Lord.
R. Who made heaven and earth.
    Glory be to the Father. . . .

HYMN

READING

Saint Paul, in his letter to the Romans, tells how we should love one another and be patient and kind to one another for the sake of Our Lord Jesus Christ who came to save us. Jesus will come again to take us with Him in glory to heaven.

May God grant you to live in such harmony with one another, in accord with Christ Jesus, that together you may with one voice glorify the God and Father of our Lord Jesus Christ. Welcome one another, therefore, as Christ has welcomed you, for the glory of God. May the God of hope fill you with all joy and peace in believing, so that by the power of the Holy Spirit you may abound in hope.

PRAYER

Stir up our minds, O Lord, with a great love for you. Grant that we may prepare for the coming of your only Son and that through His coming we may grow to serve Him in the poor and the needy, through Jesus Christ our Lord, who lives and reigns with you and the Holy Spirit, one God, world without end. Amen.

THE LORD'S PRAYER

BLESSING

May the blessing of Almighty God, the Father, the Son and the Holy Spirit, remain with us always.

60. ADVENT

V. Come, Lord Jesus! Come!

R. Come, Lord Jesus! Come.

HYMN

READING

Yesterday [Sunday] was the first day of Advent. Advent means to come near to. We are coming near to Christmas.

For a very long time—from the time when the first people had said the first "No" to God—the world had been waiting for the coming of our Lord. He was sometimes called the Messiah.

Sometimes, God's chosen people had served Him well but often they had been wicked. God had sent them men to tell them about himself and the Saviour He would send for all men, so that all men could receive God's life and love once more.

During the four weeks of Advent, we should be getting ourselves ready for Christmas, which is the birthday of Jesus, our Saviour, who was born to save us from our sins and to show us the way to God's heavenly kingdom.

We can get ourselves ready best of all by trying hard to please God. We please God best when we pray to Him, when we do as we are told, when we say the truth, when we help other people especially the poor and the needy. We please God when we think of others before ourselves, when we are cheerful when things go wrong and especially when we receive Him during Holy Mass in Communion.

Prayer, obedience, love of others—even those we do not like very much—cheerfulness, are the presents we can be saving up to offer Jesus on His birthday at Christmas.

Birthdays are for getting presents. Is our Lord

going to get these presents from us? If He does He will
be very pleased with us. If He does, He will make sure
that we have a very happy Christmas.

PRAYER

Come, Lord Jesus! Come and save us from our sins and save us
by your power. Help us to get ready to celebrate your coming so
that we may be well pleasing to God our Father. Amen.

THE LORD'S PRAYER

BLESSING

May the blessing of Him who is to come be with us now and
remain with us always. Amen.

61. ADVENT

V. Come, Lord Jesus! Come.
R. Come, Lord Jesus! Come.

HYMN

READING

Advent, as we saw yesterday, means to come near
to. We are getting near to Christmas, to the birthday of
Our Lord.

Our Lord will never again be born in a stable.

He has already come and has given us a share of
His Life at our Baptism and has come to us in the other
Sacraments. We have a share of His life of grace. And
yet He is coming and we are to get ready.

Our getting ready for Him cannot be getting ready
for His birthday. It should be a getting ready for our
birthday into heaven and for the coming of God's kingdom. Saint John's last prayer in the Bible is "Come,
Lord Jesus."

We are inviting Jesus, our Saviour, to come and to

D

take us all and to lead us to our Heavenly Father so that we can be all His. This is what we should be getting ready for at every moment of our lives. We should be trying to make ourselves all pleasing to God. Sometimes we will make mistakes, perhaps by becoming angry or by saying or doing something unkind to someone else whom our Father wants with Him in heaven. Does that unkindness perhaps make it more difficult for that person to be pleasing to God? Do we, by what we think, or say, or do, make it easy for others to please God? We are surely looking forward to every happiness in Heaven. We should be praying: "Come, Lord Jesus". Are we ready for his coming?

We do not know if the time of His coming to take us to our Father will be today or next month or in fifty years' time. We do not know, but we should be ready. If we prayed each day, "Come, Lord Jesus", we should perhaps be more ready.

Advent is a time given to us to help us to get ready. Our Masses, and Communions, our prayers, our obedience, our doing cheerfully and well all the things we don't like doing, will help us to be thankful for the first coming of our Lord at Christmas when He came to show us the way to our Father. It will help us to be ready for the time when we meet God to give Him glory for ever in Heaven. "Come, Lord Jesus, come."

PRAYER

Dear Jesus, please help us to be ready to give glory with you to God our Father. Help us to look forward to the time when we shall be taken to heaven. We can do this by showing our love for you now and by loving our neighbours for Your sake. Amen.

THE LORD'S PRAYER

BLESSING

May the blessing of Him who is to come be with us now and remain with us always. Amen.

62. ISAIAH IS CALLED TO BE A PROPHET

V. O Lord, open my lips!

R. And my mouth shall declare your praise!

Glory be to the Father. . . .

HYMN

READING

A prophet is a messenger of God. Today we shall hear how Isaiah was called to be a prophet. Isaiah knew that he was unworthy to do the work that God had for him to do, for God is so Holy. But he knew that God would help him to do his work. We read of this in the Book of Isaiah.

In the year that King Uzziah died I saw the Lord sitting upon a throne, high and lifted up; and his train filled the temple. Above him stood the seraphim; each had six wings: with two he covered his face, and with two he covered his feet, and with two he flew. And one called to another and said:

"Holy, holy, holy is the Lord of hosts;
the whole earth is full of his glory."

And the foundations of the thresholds shook at the voice of him who called, and the house was filled with smoke. And I said: "Woe is me! for I am lost; for I am a man of unclean lips, and I dwell in the midst of a people of unclean lips; for my eyes have seen the King, the Lord of hosts!"

Then flew one of the seraphim to me, having in his hand a burning coal which he had taken with tongs from the altar. And he touched my mouth, and said: "Behold, this has touched your lips; your guilt is taken away, and your sin forgiven." And I heard the voice of the Lord saying, "Whom shall I send, and who will go for us?" Then I said, "Here am I! Send me."

PRAYER

Lord, if you have anything which you want me to do—anything which will help others, or help your kingdom on earth—show me what it is, and help me to want to do it, so that I may say with Isaiah, "Here I am. Send me." I ask it for the sake of Jesus Christ our Lord. Amen.

THE LORD'S PRAYER

BLESSING

And now may the God of peace bless all that we try to do in His name, through Jesus Christ, our Lord. Amen.

63. THE MESSIAH'S COMING IS FORETOLD

V. O God, come to my assistance!
R. O Lord, make haste to help me!
  Glory be to the Father. . . .

HYMN

READING

Although the Jews had often been unfaithful to God who had been so good to them, He was always ready to help them. Isaiah's message from God to his people was that a Saviour would come to them.

The people who walked in darkness have seen a
    great light;
those who dwelt in a land of deep darkness,
    on them has light shined.
For to us a child is born,
    to us a son is given;
and the government will be upon his shoulder,
    and his name will be called
"Wonderful Counsellor, Mighty God, Everlasting
    Father, Prince of Peace."

Of the increase of his government and of peace
   there will be no end,
upon the throne of David, and over his kingdom,
   to establish it, and to uphold it
with justice and with righteousness from this time
   forth and for evermore.
The zeal of the Lord of hosts will do this.

PRAYER

Lord, you are so great and so holy and have given us all good
things. Give us a great love for you so that we may be pleasing
to you. We ask this for the sake of Jesus Christ your Son whom
you sent to be our Saviour and who now lives and reigns with you
and the Holy Spirit, world without end. Amen.

THE LORD'S PRAYER

BLESSING

O God, grant that what we have said with our lips, we may believe
in our hearts and do in our lives, for your honour and glory, world
without end. Amen.

64. COMFORT MY PEOPLE

V. I have lifted up my eyes to the hills!
R. From whence my help comes.
V. My help comes from the Lord.
R. Who made heaven and earth.
   Glory be to the Father. . . .

HYMN

READING

When things became very difficult for the Jews,
Isaiah was told to bring words of comfort to them
because God would surely help them as he will surely

71

help us when we ask Him. He will make it pleasant and easy for us to do the things He wants of us if only we will trust Him.

Comfort, comfort my people,
    says your God.
Speak tenderly to Jerusalem,
    and cry to her
that her warfare is ended,
    that her iniquity is pardoned,
that she has received from the Lord's hand
    double for all her sins.

A voice cries:
"In the wilderness prepare the way of the Lord,
    make straight in the desert a highway for our God.
Every valley shall be lifted up,
    and every mountain and hill be made low;
the uneven ground shall become level,
    and the rough places a plain.
And the glory of the Lord shall be revealed,
    and all flesh shall see it together,
    for the mouth of the Lord has spoken."

PRAYER

May the Father, the Son and the Holy Spirit, guide us in this life and may the comfort which we have from the coming of the Son on the first Christmas day give us the courage always to live our lives for God, so that at last we may be able to enjoy the never ending happiness of His kingdom through the same Christ our Lord. Amen.

THE LORD'S PRAYER

BLESSING

May the grace of our Lord Jesus Christ, and the love of God and the fellowship of the Holy Spirit, be with us all evermore. Amen.

65. THE VISION OF ZECHARIAH

V. Come, O Holy Spirit, fill the hearts of your faithful, and kindle in them the fire of your love! Send forth your Spirit and they shall be created!

R. And you will renew the face of the earth!

HYMN

READING

Many prophets had helped to prepare for the coming of Our Lord. The last of them was Saint John the Baptist. Today we hear how his father, who was very old, was told that he would have a son. This son's job would be to prepare the people for the coming of our Lord who would soon be with His people. The reading is from the Gospel according to Saint Luke.

In the days of Herod, king of Judea, there was a priest named Zechariah, of the division of Abijah; and he had a wife of the daughters of Aaron, and her name was Elizabeth. And they were both righteous before God, walking in all the commandments and ordinances of the Lord blameless.

Now while he was serving as priest before God when his division was on duty, according to the custom of the priesthood, it fell to him by lot to enter the temple of the Lord and burn incense. And the whole multitude of the people were praying outside at the hour of incense. And there appeared to him an angel of the Lord standing on the right side of the altar of incense. And Zechariah was troubled when he saw him, and fear fell upon him. But the angel said to him, "Do not be afraid, Zechariah, for your prayer is heard, and your wife Elizabeth will bear you a son, and you shall call his name John. And you will have joy and gladness, and many will rejoice at his birth. And Zechariah said to the angel, "How shall I know this? For I am an old man, and my wife is advanced in years." And the angel answered him, "I am Gabriel, who stand in the presence of God; and I was sent to speak to you, and to bring you this good news. And behold, you will be silent and unable to speak until the day that these things come to pass, because you did not believe my words, which will be fulfilled in their time." And the people were waiting for Zechariah, and they wondered at his delay in the temple. And when he came out, he could not speak to them, and they perceived that he had seen a vision in the temple.

PRAYER

Lord we thank you for sending Saint John the Baptist to prepare for the coming of our Lord. Help us to listen to his teaching, to turn our backs on anything which would displease God our Father and to keep the life of God, which we received in our Baptism, strong in us. We ask this for the sake of Jesus Christ your Son and our Saviour. Amen.

THE LORD'S PRAYER

BLESSING

May the blessing of God, the Father, the Son and the Holy Spirit, be with us now and always. Amen.

66. GOD BE MERCIFUL TO US

V. Show us, Lord, your mercy!

R. And grant us your salvation.

V. Lord, hear my prayer!

R. And let my cry come to you!

I confess to Almighty God. . . .

HYMN

READING

God is so good and we so often say "No" to what we know He wants of us. We ask that He will show us His mercy by praying Psalm 67.

May God be gracious to us and bless us
  and make His face to shine upon us,
that thy way may be known upon earth.
  thy saving power among all nations.
Let the peoples praise thee, O God;
  let all the peoples praise thee!
Let the nations be glad and sing for joy,
  for thou dost judge the peoples with equity
  and guide the nations upon earth.
Let the peoples praise thee, O God;
  let all the peoples praise thee!
The earth has yielded its increase;
  God, our God, has blessed us.
God has blessed us;
  let all the ends of the earth fear Him!

PRAYER

O Lord, be merciful to us. Forgive all our wrong doings and give
us the help today to keep away from anything which will de displeasing to you. Through Jesus Christ our Saviour and our Lord.
Amen.

THE LORD'S PRAYER

BLESSING

God be merciful to us and bless us. Give us the grace to know
what you want of us and the help to do it, for Jesus Christ's sake.
Amen.

67. "I WILL LIFT UP MY EYES
TO THE HILLS"

V. I have lifted up my eyes to the hills!
R. From whence my help comes.
V. My help comes from the Lord.
R. Who made heaven and earth.
  Glory be to the Father. . . .

HYMN

READING

We need God's help at all times. We can be quite sure that He is always ready to help us when we ask Him. Psalm 121 tells us this in some very beautiful words:

> I lift up my eyes to the hills.
> From whence does my help come?
> My help comes from the Lord,
> Who made heaven and earth.
> He will not let your foot be moved,
> He who keeps you will not slumber.
> Behold, He who keeps Israel
> will neither slumber nor sleep.
> The Lord is your keeper;
> The Lord is your shade
> on your right hand.
> The sun shall not smite you by day,
> nor the moon by night.
> The Lord will keep you from all evil;
> He will keep your life.
> The Lord will keep
> your going out and your coming in
> from this time forth and for evermore.

PRAYER

Lord we need your help, now and always. Help us never to forget you. Help us to turn to you and to think of you often in our needs. Keep us always close to you, who live and reign with your Son our Lord and the Holy Spirit, for ever and ever. Amen.

THE LORD'S PRAYER

BLESSING

Be always at our side to give us strength, O God for all our trust is in You. Amen.

68. MY HELP COMES FROM THE LORD

V. Our help is in the name of the Lord!

R. Who made heaven and earth.

I confess to Almighty God. . . .

HYMN

READING

The people of God knew that He had helped them in many difficulties and they gave thanks for His help. Today we will listen to Psalm 124 and remember how often we are helped by the goodness of God.

If it had not been the Lord who was on our side,
    let Israel now say—
if it had not been the Lord who was on our side,
    when men rose up against us,
then they would have swallowed us up alive,
    when their anger was kindled against us;
then the flood would have swept us away,
    the torrent would have gone over us;
then over us would have gone the raging waters.

Blessed be the Lord,
    who has not given us
    as prey to their teeth!
We have escaped as a bird
    from the snare of the fowlers;
the snare is broken,
    and we have escaped!
Our help is in the name of the Lord,
    who made heaven and earth.

PRAYER

Dear Father in heaven, we thank you for all the help you give to us, especially for the share in your own life and love which you

77

gave us in the Sacrament of Baptism and in the Sacraments of Penance and Holy Communion. We thank you for the help and kindness given to us by our parents, our priests, our teachers and all our friends. Help us to remember that all these helps are really from you. We ask this for the sake of Jesus Christ your Son, who lives and reigns with you and the Holy Spirit, world without end. Amen.

THE LORD'S PRAYER

BLESSING

Be with us O Lord in all that we do today and give us your blessings now and always. Amen.

69. THE STILL, SMALL VOICE

V. Blessed be the holy and undivided Trinity!
R. Now and for evermore! Amen.

HYMN

READING

The great prophet Elijah teaches us that God speaks to us best in the quiet of our own minds. We should find a few minutes each day to give Him a real chance to speak to us. The reading is from the first book of Kings.

And he arose, and ate and drank, and went in the strength of that food forty days and forty nights to Horeb the mount of God. And there he came to a cave, and lodged there; and behold, the word of the Lord came to him, and He said to him, "What are you doing here, Elijah?" He said, "I have been very jealous for the Lord, the God of hosts; for the people of Israel have forsaken thy covenant, thrown down thy altars, and slain thy prophets with the sword; and I, even I

only, am left; and they seek my life, to take it away."
And He said, "Go forth, and stand upon the mount
before the Lord." And behold, the Lord passed by, and
a great and strong wind rent the mountains, and broke
in pieces the rocks before the Lord, but the Lord was
not in the wind; and after the wind an earthquake, but
the Lord was not in the earthquake; and after the earthquake a fire, but the Lord was not in the fire; and after
the fire a still small voice.

PRAYER

Whenever we are going to do something which we know will not
please you, O Lord, give us the help to stop and listen to the still,
small voice of our conscience. Then we shall avoid displeasing you.
Fill our minds, whenever we are tempted, with thoughts of your
great goodness. Speak clearly to us so that we may have no doubts
as to what you want us to do. Through Jesus Christ our Lord.
Amen.

THE LORD'S PRAYER

BLESSING

May the Lord bless us and keep us. May the Lord make His Face
to shine on us and give us His peace, now and for evermore. Amen.

70. SEEK THE LORD

V. O God, come to my assistance!
R. Lord, make haste to help me!
Glory be to the Father. . . .

HYMN

READING

God shows His loving kindness to all those who
try to do His will. God in His goodness gives us all
things. The reading is from the Book of Isaiah.

"Seek the Lord while He may be found,
call upon Him while He is near;
let the wicked forsake his way,
and the unrighteous man his thoughts;
let him return to the Lord, that He may have
mercy on him,
and to our God, for He will abundantly
pardon.
For my thoughts are not your thoughts,
neither are your ways my ways, says the Lord.
For as the heavens are higher than the earth,
so are my ways higher than your ways
and my thoughts than your thoughts.
For as the rain and the snow come down
from heaven,
and return not thither but water the earth,
making it bring forth and sprout,
giving seed to the sower and bread to the eater,
so shall my word be that goes forth from my
mouth;
it shall not return to me empty,
but it shall accomplish that which I purpose,
and prosper in the thing for which I sent it.

PRAYER

Help us, good Lord, to seek you in all things, in the beauty of the trees and flowers, and animals and of all men and women. May we be always beautiful in your sight by keeping away from all sinful thoughts, unkind words or shameful deeds. So may we follow more closely the example of our Blessed Lady and the saints, and most especially your own example. Through Christ our Lord. Amen.

THE LORD'S PRAYER

BLESSING

May God, the Father of our Lord Jesus Christ, bless, direct and keep us and give us thankful hearts now and for evermore. Amen.

71. "THE LORD IS AT HAND"

V. Show us, Lord, your mercy!

R. And grant us your salvation.

V. Lord, hear my prayer.

R. And let me cry come to you.

Glory be to the Father. . . .

HYMN

READING

As we get nearer to Christmas we should be realising how close to us Jesus is and how happy we should always be. Listen to the lovely words Saint Paul uses in his letter to the Philippians.

Rejoice in the Lord always; again I will say, Rejoice. Let all men know your forbearance. The Lord is at hand. Have no anxiety about anything, but in everything by prayer and asking with thanksgiving, let your requests be made known to God. And the peace of God, which passes all understanding, will keep your hearts and your minds in Christ Jesus.

PRAYER

Listen to our prayers, O Lord, and may we always look forward to your coming so that at last we may enjoy the happiness of your everlasting kingdom, through Jesus Christ, our Lord. Amen.

THE LORD'S PRAYER

BLESSING

May the blessing of Him whose coming fills us with so much joy and gladness fill our thoughts and minds with all graces, now and for evermore. Amen.

72. SALVATION IS NEAR

V. Our help is in the name of the Lord.
R. Who made heaven and earth.
   I confess to Almighty God. . . .

HYMN

READING

Make no mistake about it, it is time we prepared ourselves for the coming of our Lord. Our salvation is near. Let us give up our sins and our faults, our lies and our disobedience, our quarrelling and all those things which keep us from the friendship of God. It is far better that we strengthen ourselves with the graces He has to offer so that we shall be ready for His coming.

PRAYER

O Lord, send soon Your Divine Son, to heal the sores of sin on our souls. Prepare us well for His coming so that at Christmas time we may worship Him with pure minds and sinless souls. We ask this in the name of Your Divine Son who became Man for us on the first Christmas day. Amen.

THE LORD'S PRAYER

BLESSING

May the blessing of Him who is to come, enlighten our minds and lead us to Him with pure hearts. Amen.

73. HIS NAME IS JOHN

V. Come Holy Spirit, fill the hearts of your faithful and kindle in them the fire of your love!
   Send forth your Spirit and they shall be created!
R. And you shall renew the face of the earth!

HYMN

READING

Today our reading tells of the birth of Saint John the Baptist who later was going to show the people who Jesus really was. It is from the Good News told by Saint Luke.

Now the time came for Elizabeth to be delivered, and she gave birth to a son. And her neighbours and kinsfolk heard that the Lord had shown great mercy to her, and they rejoiced with her. And on the eighth day they came to circumcise the child; and they would have named him Zechariah after his father, but his mother said, "Not so; he shall be called John." And they said to her, "None of your kindred is called by this name." And they made signs to his father, inquiring what he would have him called. And he asked for a writing tablet, and wrote, "His name is John." And they all marvelled. And immediately his mouth was opened and his tongue loosed, and he spoke, blessing God. And fear came on all their neighbours. And all these things were talked about through all the hill country of Judea; and all who heard them laid them up in their hearts, saying, "What then will this child be?" For the hand of the Lord was with him.

PRAYER

O Lord, give to your people everywhere the grace of your joys and guide us all into the way of eternal happiness through our Lord, Jesus Christ, who lives and reigns with You and the Holy Spirit, one God, world without end. Amen.

THE LORD'S PRAYER

BLESSING

O God, save us waking and guard us sleeping; that awake we may watch with Christ and asleep we may rest in peace; through Jesus Christ our Lord. Amen.

74. EMBER DAYS

V. Our help is in the name of the Lord!
R. Who made heaven and earth!
   I confess to Almighty God. . . .

HYMN

READING

The Wednesday, Friday and Saturday of this week are called Ember Days.

They are special days of prayer and penance on which the Church asks us to say extra prayers and to do special acts of penance. They are days during each of the seasons of the year on which priests are ordained.

There is a great need for more priests in many parts of the world. We should pray hard that many boys and young men will offer themselves to be priests, in answer to God's call, so that the Mass and the Sacraments will be there for people all over the world.

Let us think quietly in our own minds of all that our priests do for us and say a special prayer for more priests.

(*Pause for about half a minute—*)

> Lord, give us more priests and holy priests.
> Lord, guide and bless our bishops, especially
>   our own Bishop N......
> (Insert the name of the Bishop of your diocese.)

PRAYER

O God, whose will it is that all men should be saved and come to know the truth, we pray that you will give us more priests and holy priests that they may spread the good news of you and your coming to all mankind, through Jesus Christ our Lord. Amen.

THE LORD'S PRAYER

BLESSING

May the blessing of Almighty God, the Father, the Son and the Holy Spirit, come down on us and be with us always. Amen.

75. ZECHARIAH'S PROPHECY

V. O Lord, open my lips!
R. And my mouth will declare your praise!
   Glory be to the Father. . . .

HYMN

READING

Today we are going to listen to what Zechariah had
to say of his son John the Baptist who was to prepare
the way for our Lord's teachings. The reading is from
the Good News told by Saint Luke.

And his father Zechariah was filled with the Holy
Spirit, and prophesied, saying,

"Blessed be the Lord God of Israel,
for He has visited and redeemed His people,
And you, child, will be called the prophet of the
   Most High;
for you will go before the Lord to prepare His ways.
to give knowledge of salvation to His people
in the forgiveness of their sins,
to guide our feet into the way of peace."

And the child grew and became strong in spirit, and he
was in the wilderness till the day of his manifestation to
Israel.

PRAYER

O God, our Father in heaven, you have given us so many blessings.
Help us to be thankful for the love our parents give to us. We are
thankful too for all the help we have from our teachers and friends.
May we never be selfish nor take all this help for granted. May
we never forget you, Father, who sent your only Son to live among
men to be a light in their darkness and to guide us all to you. Amen.

THE LORD'S PRAYER

BLESSING

Bless, guide and strengthen us, your children, O Lord, and keep
us ever close to your side, for you are our strength and our Saviour.
Amen.

76. THE BIRTH OF JESUS FORETOLD

V. Come, Lord Jesus! Come!
R. Come, Lord Jesus! Come!

HYMN

READING

Today Saint Luke tells us how the Angel Gabriel told our Blessed Lady that she was to be the Mother of God.

The angel Gabriel was sent from God to a city of Galilee named Nazareth, to a virgin betrothed to a man whose name was Joseph, of the house of David; and the virgin's name was Mary. And he came to her and said, "Hail, full of grace, the Lord is with you!" But she was greatly troubled at the saying, and considered in her mind what sort of greeting this might be. And the angel said to her, "Do not be afraid, Mary, for you have found favour with God, and behold, you will conceive in your womb and bear a son, and you shall call his name Jesus. He will be great and will be called the Son of the Most High; and the Lord God will give him the throne of his father David, and He will reign over the house of Jacob for ever; and of His kingdom there will be no end."

PRAYER

Make everything that we think, or say, or do, be pleasing to you, O God. May we follow the example of our Blessed Lady by always saying "Yes" to what you want from us. So we shall always be pleasing to you, our Master and Friend, who taught us to say:

Our Father. . . .

BLESSING

May the Lord bless us and keep us. May the Lord make His face to shine on us and give us His peace now and for evermore. Amen.

77. OUR LADY GETS READY
FOR CHRISTMAS

V. Blessed art thou among women!
R. And blessed is the fruit of thy womb, Jesus!
   Glory be to the Father. . . .

HYMN

READING

We all know how exciting it is at home when we are waiting for the baby to be born. There is a lot of work to be done. There are the baby clothes to be got ready, the cot to be prepared and there is great joy and happiness. Our Lady had to get ready for the birth of her Son, our Lord. But before He was born, she found time to visit her old cousin Saint Elizabeth who was waiting for the birth of her son, who was to be Saint John the Baptist. Let us listen to Saint Luke's story of the Visitation.

In those days Mary arose and went with haste into the hill country, to a city of Judah, and she entered the house of Zechariah and greeted Elizabeth. And when Elizabeth heard the greeting of Mary, the babe leaped in her womb; and Elizabeth was filled with the Holy Spirit and she exclaimed with a loud cry, "Blessed are you among women, and blessed is the fruit of your womb! And why is this granted me, that the mother of my Lord should come to me? For behold, when the voice of your greeting came to my ears, the babe in my womb leaped for joy. And blessed is she who believed that there would be a fulfilment of what was spoken to her from the Lord." And Mary said, "My soul magnifies the Lord, and my spirit rejoices in God my Saviour."

PRAYER

Come to us O Lord, in your great goodness, that we who rely on your goodness, may quickly be saved from all harm. Through our

Lord Jesus Christ your Son, who lives and reigns with you and the Holy Spirit, world without end. Amen.

THE LORD'S PRAYER

BLESSING

May the blessing of Him who is to come be with us today and always. Amen.

78. JESUS IS BORN IN BETHLEHEM

V. And the Word was made flesh.

R. And dwelt amongst us!

I believe in God. . . .

HYMN

READING

Saint Luke tells us in a very beautiful way of the birth of our Lord.

In those days a decree went out from Caesar Augustus that all the world should be enrolled. This was the first enrolment, when Quirinius was governor of Syria. And all went to be enrolled, each to his own city. And Joseph also went up from Galilee, from the city of Nazareth, to Judea, to the city of David, which is called Bethlehem, because he was of the house and lineage of David, to be enrolled with Mary, his betrothed, who was with child. And while they were there, the time came for her to be delivered. And she gave birth to her first born son and wrapped Him in swaddling cloths, and laid Him in a manger, because there was no place for them in the inn.

PRAYER

O God, our Father, who looked after our Blessed Lady and her baby, Jesus, look after all mothers. Help them to know that you will always look after them. Help them to look after the children you have given them. We ask this for the sake of Jesus Christ your son whom you gave to our Lady in Bethlehem so that he could show us the way to you. Amen.

THE LORD'S PRAYER

BLESSING

May God the Father, God the Son, and God the Holy Spirit, bless, keep and preserve us now and always. Amen.

79. THE SHEPHERDS AND THE ANGEL

V. I have lifted up my eyes to the hills!
R. From whence my help comes.
V. My help comes from the Lord!
R. Who made heaven and earth.
  Glory be to the Father. . . .

HYMN

READING

The first to hear of the birth of our Lord were the humble shepherds. Saint Luke tells us how they heard of His birth.

"In the same country there were shepherds awake in the fields, keeping the night watches over their flocks. And all at once an angel of the Lord came and stood by them and the glory of the Lord shone around them, and they were filled with fear. And the angel said to them, "Be not afraid; for behold, I bring you good news of a great joy which will come to all the people; for to you is born this day in the city of David a Saviour, who is Christ the Lord. And this will be a sign for you: you will find a babe wrapped in swaddling cloths and lying in a manger." And suddenly there was with the angel a multitude of heavenly host praising God and saying,

"Glory to God in the highest,
and on earth peace among men with whom
He is pleased!"

When the angels went away from them into heaven, the shepherds said to one another, "Let us go over to Bethlehem and see this thing that has happened, which the Lord has made known to us." And they went with haste, and found Mary and Joseph, and the babe lying in a manger. And when they saw it they made known the saying which had been told them concerning this child; and all who heard it wondered at what the shepherds told them. But Mary kept all these things, pondering them in her heart. And the shepherds returned, glorifying and praising God for all they had heard and seen, as it had been told them.

PRAYER

O God, you sent the message of the birth of your son first of all to the humble shepherds. They were so happy to have this good news. Please help us to be happy at the message you have for us that we should love one another and show our love for you. Help us as we try in our little way to spread good-will around us and so bring nearer your reign of peace on earth. We ask it for Jesus Christ's sake. Amen.

THE LORD'S PRAYER

BLESSING

The peace of God which passes all understanding, fill our hearts and minds with the knowledge and love of God and of His Son, Jesus Christ our Lord. Amen.

80. THE VISIT OF THE WISE MEN

V. Blessed be the Holy and Undivided Trinity!
R. Now and for evermore. Amen.

HYMN

READING

After men had turned their backs on God, He chose the people of Israel to prepare for the coming of the Saviour. Then all the peoples of the world would begin to love God again. The first people who were not Jews who came to know and to love our Lord were the Wise Men. Saint Matthew tells us of this in his Good News.

Now when Jesus was born in Bethlehem of Judea in the days of Herod the king, behold, wise men from the East came to Jerusalem, saying, "Where is He who has been born king of the Jews? For we have seen His star in the East, and have come to worship Him." When Herod the king heard this, he was troubled, and all Jerusalem with him; and assembling all the chief priests and scribes of the people, he inquired of them where the Christ was to be born. They told him, "In Bethlehem of Judea; for so it is written by the prophet:
'And you, O Bethlehem, in the land of Judah,
are by no means least among the rulers of
Judah;
for from you shall come a ruler
who will govern my people Israel.' "
Then Herod summoned the wise men secretly and ascertained from them what time the star appeared; and he sent them to Bethlehem, saying, "Go and search diligently for the child, and when you have found Him bring me word, that I too may come and worship Him." When they had heard the king they went their way; and lo, the star which they had seen in the East went before them, till it came to rest over the place where the child was. When they saw the star, they rejoiced ex-

ceedingly with great joy; and going into the house they saw the child with Mary his mother, and they fell down and worshipped Him. Then, opening their treasures, they offered Him gifts, gold and frankincense and myrrh. And being warned in a dream not to return to Herod, they departed to their own country by another way.

PRAYER

Lord, we have no great gifts to offer you like the Wise men had, but we offer you what little we can. We offer you our reverence as we bow down to worship you. We offer you our thanks that we are alive and well today. We give you our love for all the kindness and help you give us. Take our little offerings, Lord, for the sake of Jesus Christ your Son, who lives and reigns with you in the unity of the Holy Spirit, world without end. Amen.

THE LORD'S PRAYER

BLESSING

Teach us good Lord, to serve you as you deserve; to give and not to count the cost; to fight and not to heed the wounds; to toil and not to seek for rest; to work for you and not to ask for any reward except to know that we are doing your will, for the sake of Jesus Christ our Lord. Amen.

81.   THE FLIGHT INTO EGYPT

V. O Lord open my lips!
R. And my mouth will declare your praise!
   Glory be to the Father. . . .

HYMN

READING

Wicked people were afraid that the coming of Jesus might make them give up their sinful ways, and so even when He was very young our Blessed Lady and Saint

Joseph had to escape from a wicked king. Saint Matthew tells us about this.

An angel of the Lord appeared to Joseph in a dream and said, "Rise, take the child and his mother, and flee to Egypt, and remain there till I tell you; for Herod is about to search for the child, to destroy Him." And he rose and took the child and his mother by night, and departed to Egypt, and remained there until the death of Herod.

PRAYER

O God, you protect all those who trust in you. Help all those who have no homes. Protect us all from all dangers to our souls and bodies so that we may be fit to reach our heavenly home with you and to live and reign with your Son and the Holy Spirit, world without end. Amen.

THE LORD'S PRAYER

BLESSING

May the Lord bless us in all that we do and keep us free from all sin, now and for evermore. Amen.

82. HEROD KILLS THE INNOCENT CHILDREN

V. Our help is in the name of the Lord!
R. Who made heaven and earth!
I confess to Almighty God. . . .

HYMN

READING

To try to make sure that he killed Jesus, Herod had many children killed. They had done no wrong. They gave their lives for Jesus. They are saints in heaven. The story of this is in Saint Matthew's Good News.

Then Herod, when he saw that he had been tricked by the wise men, was in a furious rage, and he sent and killed all the male children in Bethlehem and in all that region who were two years old or under, according to the time which he had ascertained from the wise men.

PRAYER

Dear Jesus, help us always to do things for you. If ever anything happens to us which makes us unhappy or makes us suffer, please do not let us grumble about it. Let us offer it up with you, who did so much for us. Amen.

THE LORD'S PRAYER

BLESSING

May the blessing of God the Father, God the Son, and God the Holy Spirit, be with us now and always. Amen.

83. THE RETURN TO NAZARETH

V. O God, come to my assistance.
R. O Lord, make haste to help me!
   Glory be to the Father. . . .

HYMN

READING

The reading today is from the Gospel according to Saint Matthew.

But when Herod died, behold, an angel of the Lord appeared in a dream to Joseph in Egypt, saying, "Rise, take the child and his mother, and go to the land of Israel, for those who sought the child's life are dead." And he rose and took the child and his mother, and went to the land of Israel. But when he heard that Archelaus reigned over Judea in place of his father Herod, he was afraid to go there, and being warned in a dream he withdrew to the district of Galilee. And he

went and dwelt in a city called Nazareth, that what was
spoken by the prophets might be fulfilled, "He shall be
called a Nazarene."

PRAYER

O Lord, you guided Saint Joseph on his journey out of Egypt.
Look down on us and guide all that we do today. Bless all our
parents and friends and gather us all into one great family which
will serve you faithfully in all things, through Jesus Christ our
Lord. Amen.

THE LORD'S PRAYER

BLESSING

We commit ourselves to your Fatherly care this day, O Lord. Be
near us at all times to comfort us and to give us your peace, for
ever and ever. Amen.

84. SIMEON'S SONG

V. O God, come to my assistance!
R. Lord make haste to help me!
   I confess to Almighty God. . . .

HYMN

READING

Simeon was one of the faithful Jews who was
looking forward to the coming of the Saviour. He
recognised Jesus as the Saviour when our Lady and
Saint Joseph took Him to the Temple to give thanks for
His birth.

We read of this in the Good News told by Saint
Luke.

Now there was a man in Jerusalem, whose name
was Simeon, and this man was righteous and devout,
looking for the consolation of Israel, and the Holy Spirit
was upon him. And it had been revealed to him by the

95

Holy Spirit that he should not see death before he had
seen the Lord's Christ. And inspired by the Spirit he
came into the temple; and when the parents brought in
the child Jesus, to do for him according to the custom of
the law, he took Him up in his arms and blessed God
and said,
> "Lord, now lettest thou thy servant depart in peace,
> according to thy word;
> for mine eyes have seen thy salvation
> which thou hast prepared in the presence of all
> peoples,
> a light for revelation to the Gentiles,
> and for glory to thy people Israel."

PRAYER

Dear Lord, Simeon was so thankful that he had lived to see you.
Please help us to thank you for all that you have done for us by
the coming of our Lord so that we too may at last see Him and
be with Him in your everlasting kingdom. We ask this for the sake
of Jesus Christ your Son, who lives and reigns with you and the
Holy Spirit, world without end. Amen.

THE LORD'S PRAYER

BLESSING

To God the Father, God the Son, and God the Holy Spirit, be glory
and honour for evermore. Amen.

85. THE BOYHOOD OF JESUS

V. O Lord, open my lips!
R. And my mouth shall declare your praise!
   Glory be to the Father. . . .

HYMN

READING

Saint Luke tells us how Jesus behaved at home
when He was a young boy. Perhaps the greatest lesson

our Lord has for all of us is that He was obedient to His Father always. He always did what His Father wanted. Here Saint Luke tells us that Jesus was obedient to our Lady and Saint Joseph and grew up to live a very holy life to show us an example.

And He went down with them and came to Nazareth, and was obedient to them; and His mother kept all these things in her heart.
And Jesus increased in wisdom and in stature, and in favour with God and man.

PRAYER

Dear Jesus, help us always to follow your example by being obedient to our parents and all those who have care of us ,so that we, too, may grow in favour with God and man, till we at last reach your heavenly kingdom. We ask it for your Name's sake. Amen.

THE LORD'S PRAYER

BLESSING

May the Lord bless us and keep us now and for evermore. Amen.

86. JESUS IN THE TEMPLE

V. I have lifted up my eyes to the hills!
R. From whence comes my help!
V. My help comes from the Lord!
R. Who made heaven and earth!
  I confess to Almighty God. . . .

HYMN

READING

Today, Saint Luke tells us of how Jesus was in His Father's house, the Temple. There He shows us that

Jesus wants more than anything else to do the will of His Father.

Now His parents went to Jerusalem every year at the feast of the Passover. And when he was twelve years old, they went up according to custom; and when the feast was ended, as they were returning, the boy Jesus stayed behind in Jerusalem. His parents did not know it, but supposing Him to be in the company they went a day's journey, and they sought Him among their kinsfolk and acquaintances; and when they did not find Him, they returned to Jerusalem, seeking Him. After three days they found Him in the temple, sitting among the teachers, listening to them and asking them questions; and all who heard Him were amazed at His understanding and His answers. And when they saw Him they were astonished; and his mother said to Him, "Son, why have you treated us so? Behold, your father and I have been looking for you anxiously." And He said to them, "How is it that you sought me? Did you not know that I must be in my Father's house?" And they did not understand the saying which He spoke to them.

PRAYER

Dear Jesus, help us to know what you want from us and to try our best to do it. Show us that what matters is not what we want. Help us to see that by helping others as much we can we are doing the will of our Heavenly Father. By doing this we shall at last find true happiness in our Father's house. Through Christ our Lord. Amen.

THE LORD'S PRAYER

BLESSING

Save us, O God, waking, and guard us sleeping, that awake we may watch with Christ, and asleep we may rest in peace. Amen.

87. THE MARRIAGE FEAST AT CANA

V. Our help is in the name of the Lord!
R. Who made heaven and earth.
  Glory be to the Father. . . .

HYMN

READING

Jesus had not yet begun the great work His Father had sent Him to do when He was invited to a wedding. They ran out of wine but when our Lady asked Him to help He did so and showed His power and His glory. When we are in need we should always ask our Blessed Lady to pray to her Son for us because He will always listen to His Mother. Saint John tells us this story in his Good News.

On the third day there was a marriage at Cana in Galilee, and the mother of Jesus was there; Jesus also was invited to the marriage, with his disciples. When the wine failed, the mother of Jesus said to Him, "They have no wine." And Jesus said to her, "O woman, what have you to do with me? My hour has not yet come." His mother said to the servants, "Do whatever He tells you." Now six stone jars were standing there, for the Jewish rites of purification, each holding twenty or thirty gallons. Jesus said to them, "Fill the jars with water." And they filled them up to the brim. He said to them, "Now draw some out, and take it to the steward of the feast." So they took it. When the steward of the feast tasted the water now become wine, and did not know where it came from (though the servants who had drawn the water knew), the steward of the feast called the bridegroom and said to him, "Every man serves the good wine first; and when men have drunk freely, then the poor wine; but you have kept the good wine until now." This, the first of his signs, Jesus did at Cana in Galilee, and manifested His glory; and His disciples believed in Him.

E

88. RUTH AND NAOMI

V. Blessed be the Holy and undivided Trinity!
R. Now and for evermore. Amen.

HYMN

READING

The reading today is from the Book of Ruth.

Once, long ago, a lady called Naomi had to go with her husband and two sons to a far off land because there was a famine in their own country. So Naomi settled as a stranger in a land where the people did not know God. But Naomi and her family continued to love God.

Soon Naomi's husband died. Then her two sons married girls from this strange land and after a few years the sons died too. How sad Naomi was! She was left alone in a foreign land, alone with her daughters-in-law, Orpah and Ruth.

Not long afterwards she heard that there was food in her own country and since she was living with foreigners and far from her own people she decided to go home.

She told Orpah and Ruth what she was going to do, and suggested that they go home to their mothers.

Listen now to these beautiful words from the Book of Ruth:

100

"Go, return each of you to her mother's house. May the Lord deal kindly with you, as you have dealt with the dead and with me. Then they lifted up their voices and wept again; and Orpah kissed her mother-in-law, but Ruth clung to her.

And she said, "See, your sister-in-law has gone back to her people and to her gods; return after your sister-in-law." But Ruth said, "Entreat me not to leave you or to return from following you; for where you go I will go, and where you lodge I will lodge; your people shall be my people, and your God my God; where you die I will die, and there will I be buried. May the Lord do so to me and more also if even death parts me from you."

PRAYER

Lord, help us always to be faithful to what you want us to do and to follow you wherever you lead us, for the sake of Jesus Christ our Lord. Amen.

THE LORD'S PRAYER

BLESSING

Grant, O Lord, that what we say with our lips we may believe in our hearts and practise in our lives, for your honour and glory; through Jesus Christ our Lord. Amen.

89. LOVE OUR ENEMIES

V. O God, come to my assistance!
R. Lord, make haste to help me!
   I confess to Almighty God. . . .

HYMN

READING

As Christians we should be different from other people. Everybody loves those who are good and kind to them. It is Christian to love even those who are unkind to us and who hurt us. We know this because Jesus came to take all people to His kingdom. We should help even our enemies to get there by showing a great love for them. Listen carefully to this reading from the Gospel according to Saint Matthew.

"You have heard that it was said, 'You shall love your neighbour and hate your enemy.' But I say to you, Love your enemies and pray for those who persecute you, so that you may be sons of your Father who is in heaven; for he makes His sun rise on the evil and on the good, and sends rain on the just and on the unjust. For if you love those who love you, what reward have you? Do not even the tax collectors do the same? And if you salute only your brethren, what more are you doing than others? Do not even the Gentiles do the same? You, therefore, must be perfect, as your heavenly Father is perfect.

PRAYER
Dear Jesus, give us a great love for all people and use us to help to bring them to your kingdom and to know of your great love for them, so that all may join you in loving the Father and the Holy Spirit for ever and ever. Amen.

THE LORD'S PRAYER

BLESSING
May the blessing of God, the Father, the Son, and the Holy Spirit be with us and all people now and always. Amen.

90. THE SON OF THE WIDOW OF NAIN

V. Praised be Jesus Christ!
R. Praised for evermore!
 Glory be to the Father. . . .

HYMN

READING
The reading today is from the Good News told by Saint Luke.

Soon afterward He went to a city called Nain, and His disciples and a great crowd went with Him. As He drew near to the gate of the city, behold, a man who had died was being carried out, the only son of his mother, and she was a widow; and a large crowd from the city was with her. And when the Lord saw her, He had compassion on her and said to her, "Do not weep." And He came and touched the bier, and the bearers stood still. And He said, "Young man, I say to you, arise." And the dead man sat up, and began to speak. And He gave him to his mother. Fear seized them all; and they glorified God, saying, "A great prophet has arisen among us!" And "God has visited His people!" And this report concerning Him spread through the whole of Judea and all the surrounding country.

PRAYER

Lord, we know that you can do all things. You can heal the sick and bring the dead to life and can forgive sins. We hope that you will keep us safe today from everything which may harm our souls and bodies. We ask this for the sake of Jesus Christ your Son, our Lord. Amen.

THE LORD'S PRAYER

BLESSING

Bless us, O Lord, and bless all those who have any sorrow or sadness, for the sake of Christ our Lord. Amen.

91. THE GROWING SEED

V. Blessed be the Holy and Undivided Trinity!
R. Now and for evermore. Amen.

HYMN

READING

Today's reading is from the Good News told by Saint Mark.

And he said, "The kingdom of God is as if a man should scatter seed upon the ground, and should sleep and rise night and day, and the seed should sprout and grow, he knows not how. The earth produces of itself, first the blade, then the ear, then the full grain in the ear. But when the grain is ripe, at once he puts in the sickle, because the harvest has come."

PRAYER

O God, plant in our hearts the seeds of goodness while we are young so that as we grow up we may come closer to you. Then at last we may come to your everlasting kingdom, through Christ our Lord. Amen.

THE LORD'S PRAYER

BLESSING

May God, the Father, the Son and the Holy Spirit, bless, keep and preserve us now and for evermore. Amen.

92. SAUL'S CONVERSION

V. Praised be Jesus Christ!
R. Praised for evermore! Amen.

HYMN

READING

Today Saint Luke tells us how Saul who had hated Christians met Jesus in a vision and came to love Him. The reading is from the Acts of the Apostles.

But Saul, still breathing threats and murder against the disciples of the Lord, went to the high priest and asked him for letters to the synagogues at Damascus, so that if he found any belonging to the Way, men or women, he might bring them bound to Jerusalem. Now as he journeyed he approached Damascus, and suddenly a light from heaven flashed about him. And he fell to the ground and heard a voice saying to him, "Saul, Saul, why do you persecute me?" And he said, "Who are you, Lord?" And He said, "I am Jesus, whom you are persecuting; but rise and enter the city, and you will be told what you are to do." The men who were travelling with him stood speechless, hearing the voice but seeing no one. Saul arose from the ground; and when his eyes were opened, he could see nothing; so they led him by the hand and brought him into Damascus. And for three days he was without sight, and neither ate nor drank.

Now there was a disciple at Damascus named Ananias. The Lord said to him in a vision, "Ananias." And he said, "Here I am, Lord." And the Lord said to him, "Rise and go to the street called Straight, and inquire in the house of Judas for a man of Tarsus named Saul; for behold, he is praying, and he has seen a man named Ananias come in and lay his hands on him so that he might regain his sight."

So Ananias departed and entered the house. And laying his hands on him he said, "Brother Saul, the Lord Jesus who appeared to you on the road by which you came, has sent me that you may regain your sight and be filled with the Holy Spirit." And immediately something like scales fell from his eyes and he regained his sight. Then he rose and was baptized.

PRAYER

Lord, grant that all men may come to know you and to love you, no matter how far away from you they are. Help them as you helped Saul so that we may all be with you at last in your kingdom. Through Christ our Lord. Amen.

THE LORD'S PRAYER

BLESSING

O God, be always near to us to guide our hearts and minds in your ways. Through Jesus Christ our Lord. Amen.

93. A CELEBRATION FOR CANDLEMAS

V. He is the light which shall give revelation to the Gentiles!
R. He is the glory of your people Israel!

HYMN

O Christ, we know you are the light upon our way.
We will follow you and reach our Father's home one day.

Reader 1

At this time there was man named Simeon living in Jerusalem who waited patiently for comfort to be brought to Israel. The Holy Spirit was with him and by the Holy Spirit he had learned that he would not die until he had seen that Christ whom the Lord had anointed. Led by the Spirit, Simeon came into the Temple and when the child Jesus was brought in by his parents, Simeon too, was able to take Him in his arms.

Sing verse—O Christ we know . . .

Light Candles. (If possible all children should hold a lighted candle, but prudence and circumstances will dictate this.)

Reader 2

Holy Lord, we wish to carry these lights in our hands in your honour. We wish to praise you in song. Please listen to us, Lord. Make our hearts burn with love for you, and for all people, who are our neighbours. May we love you so well that we may be worthy to be with you for ever, in heaven.

Sing verse—O Christ we know . . .

Reader 3

Lord Jesus Christ, grant that as these candles can light up the dark, so may our souls always be on fire for love of you. Do not let the darkness of sin take away the light of your grace. May we be worthy to reach our home in heaven where we shall live for ever in the light of your love. We ask this through you, Christ

106

Jesus, the Saviour of the world, who are God, living and reigning with the Father and the Holy Spirit, one God, God, world without end. Amen.

Sing verse—O Christ we know ...

Reader 4

Lord Jesus Christ, whom the aged Simeon recognised as our Saviour, grant that we may have the gift of the Holy Spirit and that we may love you more each day of our lives.

Sing verse—O Christ we know ...

Chorus

He is the light which shall give revelation to the Gentiles,
He is the glory of your people Israel!

Reader 5

Lord, now dost Thou let Thy servant go in peace, according to Thy promise.

Chorus

He is the light which shall give revelation to the Gentiles,
He is the glory of your people Israel!

Reader 5

For my own eyes have seen that saving power of yours.

Chorus

He is the light which shall give revelation to the Gentiles,
He is the glory of your people Israel!

Reader 5

Which you have prepared in the sight of all nations!

Chorus

He is the light which shall give revelation to the Gentiles,
He is the glory of your people Israel!

Glory be to the Father and to the Son and to the Holy Spirit.

Chorus

He is the light which shall give revelation to the Gentiles,
He is the glory of your people Israel!

Reader 5

As it was in the beginning, is now and ever shall be, world without end. Amen.

Chorus

He is the light which shall give revelation to the Gentiles,
He is the glory of your people Israel!

HYMN

BLESSING

May Christ our Saviour, the light of the world, fill our hearts and minds with His love and joy and may He bring us at last to our Father's home in heaven.

94. FORGIVENESS

V. O God, come to my assistance!
R. O Lord, make haste to help me!
    Glory be to the Father. . . .

HYMN

READING

The reading today is from the Good News told by Saint Matthew.

Then Peter came up and said to him, "Lord, how often shall my brother sin against me, and I forgive him? As many as seven times?" Jesus said to him, "I do not say to you seven times, but seventy times seven.

"Therefore the kingdom of heaven may be compared to a king who wished to settle accounts with his servants. When he began the reckoning, one was brought to him who owed him ten thousand talents; and as he could not pay, his lord ordered him to be sold, with his wife and children and all that he had, and payment to be made. So the servant fell on his knees, imploring him, 'Lord, have patience with me, and I will pay you everything.' And out of pity for him the lord of that servant released him and forgave him the debt. But that same servant, as he went out, came upon one of his fellow servants who owed him a hundred denarii; and seizing him by the throat he said, 'Pay what you owe.' So his fellow servant fell down and besought him; 'Have patience with me, and I will pay you.' He refused and went and put him in prison till he should pay the debt. When his fellow servants saw what had taken place, they were greatly distressed, and they went and reported to their lord all that had taken place. Then his lord summoned him and said to him. 'You wicked servant! I forgave you all that debt because you besought me; and should not you have had mercy on your fellow servant, as I had mercy on you?' And in anger his lord delivered him to the jailers, till he should pay all his debt. So also my heavenly Father will do to every one of you, if you do not forgive your brother from your heart."

PRAYER

Lord, we often ask you to forgive us. Help us to forgive all who may do us any harm so that we may always follow the teaching of your Son, Jesus Christ, our Lord. Amen.

THE LORD'S PRAYER

BLESSING

May the love of the Father, the grace of the Son, and the fellowship and gifts of the Holy Spirit, be with us all evermore. Amen.

95. THE POWER OF GOD

V. O Lord, open my lips!

R. And my mouth shall declare your praise!

Glory be to the Father. . . .

HYMN

READING

The reading today is taken from the Gospel according to Saint Matthew.

And getting into a boat He crossed over and came to His own city. And behold, they brought to him a paralytic, lying on his bed; and when Jesus saw their faith he said to the paralytic, "Take heart, my son; your sins are forgiven." And behold, some of the scribes said to themselves, "This man is blaspheming." But Jesus, knowing their thoughts, said, "Why do you think evil in your hearts? For which is easier, to say, 'Your sins are forgiven,' or to say, 'Rise and walk'? But that you may know that the Son of man has authority on earth to forgive sins"—He then said to the paralytic—"Rise, take up your bed and go home." And he rose and went home. When the crowds saw it, they were afraid, and they glorified God, who had given such authority to men.

PRAYER

O God, you are so powerful that you can calm a storm, heal a sick person or bring the dead to life. Give me all the help I need to keep away from what is wrong and evil. Help me to do good and to be a good example to all those who are near me. Through Jesus Christ our Lord. Amen.

THE LORD'S PRAYER

BLESSING

Save us, O Lord, waking, and guard us sleeping, that awake we may watch with Christ, and asleep we may rest in peace. Amen.

96. THE LOST SHEEP

V. I have lifted up my eyes to the hills!

R. From whence my help comes.

V. My help comes from the Lord!

R. Who made heaven and earth!

   I confess to almighty God. . . .

HYMN

READING

Today's reading is from the Good News told by Saint Luke.

So he told them this parable: "What man of you, having a hundred sheep, if he has lost one of them, does not leave the ninety-nine in the wilderness, and go after the one which is lost, until he finds it? And when he has found it, he lays it on his shoulders, rejoicing. And when he comes home, he calls together his friends and his neighbours, saying to them, 'Rejoice with me, for I have found my sheep which was lost.' Just so, I tell you, there will be more joy in heaven over one sinner who repents than over ninety-nine righteous persons who need no repentance.

PRAYER

Lord, if ever we become lost to you through saying "No" to You, let us hear your voice and quickly return to your friendship. Help us to be sorry for our fault because above all else we shall have turned away from the goodness of your love for us. Through Christ our Lord. Amen.

THE LORD'S PRAYER

BLESSING

May we grow in the grace and knowledge of our Lord and Saviour Jesus Christ, to whom be honour and glory both now and forever. Amen.

97. THE LITTLE DAUGHTER OF JAIRUS

V. Praised be Jesus Christ!
R. Praised for ever more!

HYMN

READING

The reading is from the Gospel according to Saint Mark. We are shown here that Jesus came to help not only the chosen people of Israel but also all those who believe in Him.

While he was still speaking, there came from the ruler's house some who said, "Your daughter is dead. Why trouble the Teacher any further?" But ignoring what they said, Jesus said to the ruler of the synagogue, "Do not fear, only believe." And he allowed no one to follow him except Peter and James and John the brother of James. When they came to the house of the ruler of the synagogue, he saw a tumult, and people weeping and wailing loudly. And when He had entered, He said to them, "Why do you make a tumult and weep? The child is not dead but sleeping." And they laughed at Him. But He put them all outside, and took the child's father and mother and those who were with Him, and went in where the child was. Taking her by the hand He said to her, "Talitha cumi"; which means, "Little girl, I say to you, arise." And immediately the girl got up and walked; for she was twelve years old. and immediately they were overcome with amazement.

PRAYER

Dear Lord, bring help and comfort to all those who are in trouble, in sorrow or sickness especially those from our school and in our parish. Your blessing will give them courage, comfort and peace. We ask this for the sake of Jesus Christ your Son, who lives and reigns with you and the Holy Spirit, for ever and ever. Amen.

THE LORD'S PRAYER

BLESSING

May the love of our Lord draw us to Himself; may the power of our Lord give us strength in doing what He wants of us; may the joy of our Lord fill our souls; and may the blessing of God, the Father, the Son, and the Holy Spirit be with us all evermore. Amen.

98. THE RICH MAN

V. O Lord, open my lips!
R. And my mouth shall declare your praise!
Glory be to the Father. . . .

HYMN

READING

Zacchaeus had not been very pleasing to God. He had heard of Jesus and wondered what Jesus may have to say to him. Jesus showed him that He is always ready to forgive those who are sorry. Jesus came to help all sinners for He wants all to love Him and to be happy with Him in heaven. The story is told by Saint Luke.

He entered Jericho and was passing through. And there was a man named Zacchaeus; he was a chief tax collector, and rich. And he sought to see who Jesus was, but could not, on account of the crowd, because he was small of stature. So he ran on ahead and climbed up into a sycamore tree to see Him, for He was to pass that way. And when Jesus came to the place, He looked up and said to Him, "Zacchaeus, make haste and come down; for I must stay at your house today." So he made haste and came down, and received Him joyfully. And when they saw it they all murmured, "He has gone in to be the guest of a man who is a sinner." And Zacchaeus stood and said to the Lord, "Behold, Lord, the half of my goods I give to the poor; and if I have defrauded any one of anything, I restore it four-fold." And Jesus said to him, "Today salvation has come to this house, since he also is a son of Abraham. For the Son of man came to seek and to save the lost."

PRAYER

Dear Jesus, help us to know that we can do nothing without the help of your grace. Help us not to think we are more pleasing to you than anyone else. Help us to use the gifts you have given us for your honour and glory. Amen.

THE LORD'S PRAYER

BLESSING

May we have the grace of courage and gaiety, and all the blessings that come from the Father to His children. Amen.

99. O LORD, HOW MAJESTIC IS YOUR NAME

V. Blessed be the Holy and Undivided Trinity!
R. Now and for evermore! Amen.

HYMN

READING

Psalm 8 is a lovely song which tells us of the glory of God who made all things, especially man whom He made to have a share of His life and love.

> O Lord, our Lord,
>> how majestic is Thy name in all the earth!
> Thou whose glory above the heavens is chanted
>> by the mouth of babes and infants,
> Thou hast founded a bulwark because of Thy foes,
>> to still the enemy and the avenger.
> When I look at Thy heavens, the work of Thy
>> fingers,
>> the moon and the stars which Thou hast
>> established;
> what is man that Thou art mindful of him,
>> and the son of man that Thou dost care for him?

Yet Thou hast made Him little less than God,
and dost crown Him with glory and honour.
Thou hast given Him dominion over the works
Thou hast put all things under His feet,
all sheep and oxen,
and also the beasts of the field,
the birds of the air, and the fish of the sea,
whatever passes along the paths of the sea.
O Lord, our Lord,
how majestic is Thy name in all the earth!

PRAYER

Dear Father in heaven, we thank you for the sun that warms us and the air that gives us life. We thank you for all the beauty of the earth in the hills and clouds and the great machines which men have made. We thank you for our homes and our healthy bodies and minds and for the example of many brave and holy men and women. We thank you especially for the example of Jesus who came to show us how to be pleasing to you. Amen.

THE LORD'S PRAYER

BLESSING

May the Lord forgive what we have been. May He make us holy and pleasing to Him today and always. Amen.

100. THE TREASURE AND THE PEARL

V. Our help is in the name of the Lord!
R. Who made heaven and earth!
Glory be to the Father. . . .

HYMN

READING

This story which our Lord told, shows us that the most sensible thing to do is to try to get the treasure He has for us in heaven. We read this story from Saint Matthew's Gospel.

"The kingdom of heaven is like treasure hidden in a field, which a man found and covered up; then in his joy he goes and sells all that he has and buys that field.

"Again, the kingdom of heaven is like a merchant in search of fine pearls, who, on finding one pearl of great value, went and sold all that he had and bought it."

PRAYER

Lord, you have given us the precious gift of knowing you. Please help us to love you. Help those who are trying to spread your word and who are working for you. Help us to work for you in all that we think or say or do since we know that anything that does not take us towards your kingdom is worth nothing. We ask this for Jesus Christ's sake. Amen.

THE LORD'S PRAYER

BLESSING

May the Lord grant us His blessing and fill our hearts with His joy and peace. Amen.

101. THE PARABLE OF THE TALENTS

V. I have lifted up my eyes to the hills!
R. From whence my help comes.
V. My help comes from the Lord!
R. Who made heaven and earth!
    Glory be to the Father. . . .

HYMN

READING

The story which our Lord tells us in the Gospel according to Saint Matthew teaches us to use whatever God has given us as well as we possibly can.

"For it will be as when a man going on a journey called his servants and entrusted to them his property; to one he gave five talents, to another two, to another one, to each according to his ability. Then he went away. He who had received the five talents went at once and traded with them; and he made five talents more. So also, he who had the two talents made two talents more. But he who had received the one talent went and dug in the ground and hid his master's money. Now after a long time the master of those servants came and settled accounts with them. And he who had received the five talents came forward, bringing five talents more, saying, 'Master, you delivered to me five talents; here I have made five talents more.' His master said to him, 'Well done, good and faithful servant; you have been faithful over a little, I will set you over much; enter into the joy of your master.' And he also who had the two talents came forward, saying, 'Master, you delivered to me two talents; here I have made two talents more.' His master said to him, 'Well done, good and faithful servant; you have been faithful over a little, I will set you over much; enter into the joy of your master.' He also who had received the one talent came forward, saying, 'Master, I knew you to be a hard man, reaping where you did not sow, and gathering where you did not winnow; so I was afraid, and I went and hid your talent in the ground. Here you have what is yours.' But his master answered him, 'Then you ought to have invested my money with the bankers, and at my coming I should have received what was my own with interest. So take the talent from him, and give it to him who has the ten talents. For to every one who has will more be given, and he will have abundance; but from him who has not, even what he has will be taken away. And cast the worthless servant into the outer darkness; there men will weep and gnash their teeth.' "

PRAYER

O God, you have given to each one of us something that is worthwhile. Grant that we may use the gifts you have given us for you and for our fellow men, so that at the Last Day we shall be able to hear you say to us, "Well done, good and faithful servant." We ask it in the name of Jesus Christ our Lord. Amen.

THE LORD'S PRAYER

BLESSING

Send your blessings to us, O Lord, so that we may be yours for ever. Amen.

102. OUR LADY OF LOURDES

V. Blessed art thou among women!
R. And blessed is the fruit of thy womb, Jesus!

HYMN

READING

Just over a hundred years ago there lived a little girl called Bernadette.

Bernadette was not a clever girl and her mother and father were very poor, but they taught her to love God our Father and Mary, the Mother of Jesus.

One day when Bernadette was out looking for wood to make a fire in her poor home, Our Lady appeared to her. Our Lady sometimes shows herself to people when Our Lord has a special message for us, or when she sees that we are not loving God enough.

She showed herself to this little girl several times and gave her messages for us. One of the messages Our Lady sent was to tell us to pray more. She asked us to say the Rosary often. Our Lady, who appeared to St. Bernadette at Lourdes, also wants us to do more penance. Let us think of a little penance we can do each day to make up for our sins.

Many sick people have been cured at Lourdes. The sick also need our prayers.

Those who do a lot for Our Lord get many graces through His Mother. Whatever prayers and penances we do for other people is most pleasing to Our Lord. Let us pray every day for the sick, for our priest, for our parents, for our friends, and all those who need our help.

Our Lady of Lourdes, pray for us. St. Bernadette, pray for us.

PRAYER

Dear Lady of Lourdes, who taught Saint Bernadette that we should pray more and do more penance, help us to listen to your message for us. Help us to come nearer to our Blessed Lord and to God our Heavenly Father. We ask this, dear Mother, for the sake of Jesus Christ your Son who lives and reigns with God the Father and the Holy Spirit, world without end. Amen.

THE LORD'S PRAYER

BLESSING

May the blessing you gave to your blessed Mother come to us, O Lord, so that we may enjoy with her the happiness of heaven. Amen.

103. THE TEN LEPERS

V. O God, come to my assistance.
R. Lord make haste to help me!
   I confess to Almighty God. . . .

HYMN

READING

The story we are going to hear today should remind us of God's goodness to us and of how often we forget to say "Thank You". The story is told by Saint Luke.

On the way to Jerusalem he was passing along between Samaria and Galilee. And as he entered a village, he was met by ten lepers, who stood at a distance and lifted up their voices and said, "Jesus, Master, have mercy on us." When he saw them he said to them, "Go and show yourselves to the priests." And as they went they were cleansed. Then one of them, when he saw that he was healed, turned back, praising God with a

119

loud voice; and he fell on his face at Jesus' feet, giving
Him thanks. Now he was a Samaritan. Then said Jesus,
"Were not ten cleansed? Where are the nine? Was no
one found to return and give praise to God except this
foreigner?" And He said to him, "Rise and go your
way; your faith has made you well."

PRAYER

Thank you, Lord, for all your great gifts to us. Teach us to love
your commandments because you have given them to us, to show
us how to love you. If we love you we shall be able to praise you
and be with you forever in your heavenly kingdom. Amen.

THE LORD'S PRAYER

BLESSING

May grace, mercy and peace from the Father ,the Son and the Holy
Spirit be with us all this day and always. Amen.

104. THE WHEAT AND THE WEEDS

V. O God, open my lips!
R. And my mouth will declare your praise!
 Glory be to the Father. . . .

HYMN

READING

Today our Lord teaches us that He will reward us
all in the end just as we deserve. The reading is from
the Good News told by Saint Matthew.

Another parable He put before them, saying, "The
kingdom of heaven may be compared to a man who
sowed good seed in his field; but while men were sleeping, his enemy came and sowed weeds among the wheat,
and went away. So when the plants came up and bore
grain, then the weeds appeared also. And the servants
of the house-holder came and said to him, 'Sir, did you

not sow good seed in your field? How then has it weeds?' He said to them, 'An enemy has done this.' The servants said to him, 'Then do you want us to go and gather them?' But he said, 'No; lest in gathering the weeds you root up the wheat along with them. Let both grow together until the harvest; and at harvest time I will tell the reapers, Gather the weeds first and bind them in bundles to be burned, but gather the wheat into my barn.'

PRAYER

Teach us, good Lord, to serve you as you deserve; to give and not to count the cost; to fight for you and not to heed the wounds; to work for you and not to ask for any reward unless it is that we know we are doing what you want of us, through Christ our Lord. Amen.

THE LORD'S PRAYER

BLESSING

O God, be with us today and every day. Guide us in what we do and bring us at last to your eternal rest through Jesus Christ, our Lord. Amen.

105. THE SOWER

V. Praised be Jesus Christ!
R. Praised for ever more!
   Glory be to the Father. . . .

HYMN

READING

Today's reading is from the Good News told by Saint Luke.

And when a great crowd came together and people from town after town came to Him, He said in a parable: "A sower went out to sow his seed; and as he sowed, some fell along the path, and was trodden under foot, and the birds of the air devoured it. And some fell on the rock; and as it grew up, it withered away, because it had no moisture. And some fell among thorns; and the thorns grew with it and choked it. And some fell into good soil and grew, and yielded a hundredfold." As He said this, He called out, "He who has ears to hear, let him hear."

And when His disciples asked Him what this parable meant, he said, "To you it has been given to know the secrets of the kingdom of God; but for others they are in parables, so that seeing they may not see, and hearing they may not understand. Now the parable is this: The seed is the word of God. The ones along the path are those who have heard; then the devil comes and takes away the word from their hearts, that they may not believe and be saved. And the ones on the rock are those who, when they hear the word, receive it with joy; but these have no root, they believe for a while and in time of temptation fall away. And as for what fell among the thorns, they are those who hear, but as they go on their way they are choked by the cares and riches and pleasures of life, and their fruit does not mature. And as for that in the good soil, they are those who, hearing the word, hold it fast in an honest and good heart, and bring forth fruit with patience."

PRAYER

Dear Jesus, help us always to listen well to your words when they are read to us at Holy Mass or at Assembly in school, so that we may become more like you. May we always give good example so that we may draw other people to know you, to love you and to serve you. Then we will be well pleasing to our heavenly Father who with you and the Holy Spirit, lives and reigns world without end. Amen.

THE LORD'S PRAYER

BLESSING

May the blessing of God, the Father, the Son, and the Holy Spirit be with us now and always. Amen.

106. CHARITY

V. O Lord, open my lips!
R. And my mouth will declare your praise.
   Glory be to the Father. . . .

HYMN

READING

Charity is another name for love. Today, in the first letter to the Corinthians, Saint Paul tells us what real love is.

If I speak in the tongues of men and of angels, but have not love, I am a noisy gong or a clanging cymbal. And if I have prophetic powers, and understand all mysteries and all knowledge, and if I have all faith, so as to remove mountains, but have not love, I am nothing. If I give away all I have, and if I deliver my body to be burned, but have not love, I gain nothing.

Love is patient and kind; love is not jealous or boastful; it is not arrogant or rude. Love does not insist on its own way; it is not irritable or resentful; it does not rejoice at wrong, but rejoices in the right. Love bears all things, believes all things, hopes all things, endures all things.

Love never ends; as for prophecies, they will pass away; as for tongues, they will cease; as for knowledge, it will pass away. For our knowledge is imperfect and our prophecy is imperfect; but when the perfect comes, the imperfect will pass away. When I was a child, I spoke like a child, I thought like a child, I reasoned like a child; when I became a man, I gave up childish ways. For now we see in a mirror dimly, but then face to face. Now I know in part; then I shall understand fully, even as I have been fully understood. So faith, hope, love abide, these three; but the greatest of these is love.

PRAYER

Help us, Lord, to have a true love towards others. May we always try to help all we meet, even though it means putting ourselves out to do it. Help us to forgive anyone who does us wrong and to try never to offend anyone. Grant this, O Father, for the sake of Jesus Christ your Son, our Lord. Amen.

THE LORD'S PRAYER

BLESSING

Bless, guide and strengthen us, your children and keep us always on the way that leads to your everlasting kingdom, through Jesus Christ, our Saviour and Lord. Amen.

107. THE BLIND BEGGAR

V. O Lord, open my lips!
R. And my mouth will declare your praise!
    Glory be to the Father. . . .

HYMN

READING

Saint Luke tells the story of how our Lord healed the blind beggar.

As He drew near to Jericho, a blind man was sitting by the roadside begging; and hearing a multitude going by, he inquired what this meant. They told him, "Jesus of Nazareth is passing by." And he cried, "Jesus, Son of David, have mercy on me!" And those who were in front rebuked him, telling him to be silent; but he cried out all the more, "Son of David, have mercy on me!" And Jesus stopped, and commanded him to be brought to Him; and when he came near, He asked him, "What do you want me to do for you?" He said, "Lord, let me receive my sight." And Jesus said to him, "Receive your sight; your faith has made you well." And immediately he received his sight and followed Him, glorifying God; and all the people, when they saw it, gave praise to God.

PRAYER

Thank you God, for the gift of sight, and for all the beautiful things we can see around us—beautiful trees, flowers, buildings, birds and animals. May all the beauty that we see help us to think of you and to thank you for your many blessings. Through Jesus Christ our Lord. Amen.

THE LORD'S PRAYER

BLESSING

May the love of the Father, the grace of the Son, and the gifts of the Holy Spirit, be with us all evermore. Amen.

108. RETURN TO YOUR GOD

V. Our help is in the name of the Lord.
R. Who made heaven and earth.
   I confess to Almighty God. . . .

HYMN

READING

The prophet Joel gives us the message from God that no matter how much we may have offended God. He is always waiting to take us back to the friendship of His love.

"Yet even now," says the Lord,
   "return to me with all your heart,
with fasting, with weeping, and with mourning;
   and rend your hearts and not your garments."
Return to the Lord, your God,
   for He is gracious and merciful,
slow to anger, and abounding in steadfast love.

PRAYER

O my God, because you are so good, I am very sorry for ever having offended you and by the help of your grace I will never offend you again. Amen.

THE LORD'S PRAYER

BLESSING

May the blessing of God, the Father, the Son, and the Holy Spirit,
be with us all now and always. Amen.

109.   TREASURE IN HEAVEN

V. Blessed be the holy and undivided Trinity!
R. Now and for evermore. Amen.

HYMN

READING

All the things which we have now will be nothing
compared with the treasure God will give us in Heaven.
Listen to the words from the Good News told by Saint
Matthew.

"Do not lay up for yourselves treasures on earth,
where moth and rust consume and where thieves break
in and steal, but lay up for yourselves treasures in
heaven, where neither moth nor rust consumes and
where thieves do not break in and steal. For where your
treasure is, there will your heart be also.

PRAYER

Dear God, you keep watch over us at all times and are ready to
help us whenever we call on you. Help us especially in times of
danger. Give us strength when we want to say "No" to you so
that at last we may enjoy the treasures you have for us in your
everlasting kingdom. Through Christ our Lord. Amen.

THE LORD'S PRAYER

BLESSING

To God the Father, who first loved us and gave us a share in his
own life and love, to Jesus Christ His Son, who saved us from
our sins, and to God the Holy Spirit, the Comforter, be all praise
and glory, now and for ever. Amen.

110. THE LOAVES AND FISHES

V. O Sacrament most holy! O sacrament Divine!
R. All praise and all thanksgiving be every moment thine!

HYMN

READING

Jesus fed the people with a few little loaves and fishes and when they had all had sufficient there was enough left over to feed many more. He gives Himself to us in Holy Communion and wishes to give Himself to all. The reading today is from the Gospel according to Saint Matthew.

Then Jesus called His disciples to Him and said, "I have compassion on the crowd, because they have been with me now three days, and have nothing to eat; and I am unwilling to send them away hungry, lest they faint on the way." And the disciples said to him, "Where are we to get bread enough in the desert to feed so great a crowd?" And Jesus said to them, "How many loaves have you?" They said, "Seven, and a few small fish." And commanding the crowd to sit down on the ground, He took the seven loaves and the fish, and having given thanks He broke them and gave them to the disciples, and the disciples gave them to the crowds. And they all ate and were satisfied; and they took up seven baskets full of the broken pieces left over. Those who ate were four thousand men, besides women and children.

PRAYER

Dear Jesus, we thank you for this great miracle. We thank you too, for the greater miracle of giving yourself to us in Holy Communion. Help us to receive you often so that with all your people gathered around your table at this Sacred Meal we may all become more like you, and more pleasing to our Father in heaven. Amen.

THE LORD'S PRAYER

127

BLESSING

Bless, O Lord, our homes, our parents and friends and all those we
love, now and always. Amen.

111. WHATEVER A MAN SOWS

V. O God, come to my assistance!

R. Lord, make haste to help me!

I confess, to Almighty God. . . .

HYMN

READING

In his letter to the Galatians, Saint Paul reminds us
that God will give us the reward we deserve.

Do not be deceived; God is not mocked, for whatever a man sows, that he will also reap. And let us not
grow weary in well-doing, for in due season we shall
reap, if we do not lose heart. So then, as we have
opportunity, let us do good to all men.

PRAYER

Help us, Lord, to do all things for you. Show us that we can do
your will while we are at school, by doing whatever we are asked
in our lessons or our games as well as we can, and without
grumbling. We ask this through Jesus Christ our Lord. Amen.

V. Lord! Hear my prayer!

R. And let my cry come to you.

THE LORD'S PRAYER

BLESSING

Look down on us as we gather together here, O God, and bless all
that we do in your name. Through Christ our Lord. Amen.

112. WHAT DEEDS ARE COUNTED

V. O Lord, open my lips!
R. And my mouth shall declare your praise!
   Glory be to the Father. . . .

HYMN

READING

God will not forget any little thing that we do for Him. He tells us that the best way to help Him is to take care of our neighbour whom we should love as much as we love ourselves. Saint Matthew tells us what really counts in the Good News.

"When the Son of man comes in His glory, and all the angels with Him, then He will sit on His glorious throne.

"Before Him will be gathered all the nations, and He will separate them one from another as a shepherd separates the sheep from the goats, and He will place the sheep at His right hand, but the goats at the left. Then the King will say to those at His right hand, 'Come, O blessed of my Father, inherit the kingdom prepared for you from the foundation of the world; for I was hungry and you gave me food, I was thirsty and you gave me drink, I was a stranger and you welcomed me, I was naked and you clothed me, I was sick and you visited me, I was in prison and you came to me.' Then the righteous will answer Him, 'Lord, when did we see Thee hungry and feed Thee, or thirsty and give Thee drink? And when did we see Thee a stranger and welcome Thee, or naked and clothe Thee? And when did we see Thee sick or in prison and visit Thee? And the King will answer them, 'Truly I say to you, as you did it to one of the least of these my brethren, you did it to me.' "

PRAYER

Dear God, never let us look down on others who are not so fortunate as we are—those who perhaps are less clever, or not so strong and well looked after as we are. Help us to help anyone, whenever we get the chance. Fill us with love for all people for you love them all. We ask this for the sake of Jesus Christ your Son, our Lord. Amen.

THE LORD'S PRAYER

BLESSING

God, bless our homes, our parents, our teachers and all our friends, and give us your peace, now and always. Amen.

113. THE NARROW GATE

V. I will lift up my eyes to the hills!
R. From whence my help comes.
V. My help comes from the Lord!
R. Who made heaven and earth!
Glory be to the Father. . . .

HYMN

READING

The reading today is from the Gospel according to Saint Matthew.

"Enter by the narrow gate; for the gate is wide and the way is easy, that leads to destrucion, and those who enter by it are many. For the gate is narrow and the way is hard, that leads to life, and those who find it are few."

PRAYER

Dear Jesus, we know that it is a narrow gate the sheep have to use to get into the safety of the sheep fold. Show us the sure way to get to heaven by giving us a great love for your loving commandments which you gave us to guide us to the safety of your kingdom. Amen.

THE LORD'S PRAYER

May the Lord defend us and keep us safe in body and soul. Amen.

114. "LET MY PEOPLE GO"

V. O God, come to my assistance!
R. O Lord, make haste to help me!
    Glory be to the Father. . . .

HYMN

READING

When the Israelites were in Egypt they were slaves for a long time. At last the time came for God to show them and the Egyptians what a powerful God He was. He sent His servant Moses to Pharaoh with a message, "Thus says the Lord God of Israel, 'Let my people go, that they may hold a feast to me in the wilderness'. But Pharaoh did not let them go until he had been asked several times.

God loved Israel with a special love because Abraham had left all things to please God and He had promised Abraham that He would make a great nation of his children and give them a land. God loves us with a special love now, and He has promised us that we shall share the kingdom of heaven with Him if we will do the things which please Him. He has saved us by sending His own Son who died for our sins and has shown us the way to His kingdom.

PRAYER

O God, help us to be your special chosen people by loving you and by loving our neighbour by helping him whenever we can. Help us especially when we do not feel like putting ourselves out for others. We ask this for the sake of Jesus Christ our Lord whom you sent and who died that we may praise you forever in your kingdom. Amen.

THE LORD'S PRAYER

BLESSING

O God, bless all those who are dear to us and keep them safe in your love. Amen.

115. "THEY THAT GO DOWN TO THE SEA IN SHIPS"

V. Our help is in the name of the Lord!
R. Who made heaven and earth.
  Glory be to the Father. . . .

HYMN

READING

Psalm 107 is a hymn thanking God for His great power and mercy, to those who trust in Him. Verses 23 to 31 ask for help for seamen. We should remember too, all those who travel.

Some went down to the sea in ships,
  doing business on the great waters;
they saw the deeds of the Lord,
  his wondrous works in the deep.
For He commanded, and raised the stormy wind,
  which lifted up the waves of the sea.
They mounted up to heaven, they went down to the
    depths;
  their courage melted away in their evil plight;
they reeled and staggered like drunken men,
  and were at their wits' end.
Then they cried to the Lord in their trouble,
  and He delivered them from their distress;
He made the storm be still,
  and the waves of the sea were hushed.
Then they were glad because they had quiet,
  and He brought them to their desired haven.
Let them thank the Lord for His steadfast love,
  for his wonderful works to the sons of men!

132

PRAYER

Today we ask you, Lord, to help all those who are seamen and who face the dangers of the sea. Help them in your mercy and guide them safely to port. Guide all your people, Lord, that they all may make a safe journey towards your heavenly kingdom, through Jesus Christ our Lord. Amen.

THE LORD'S PRAYER

BLESSING

May God the Father, God the Son and God the Holy Spirit bless us and keep us in His safe care now and always. Amen.

116. THE PRODIGAL SON

V. O Lord open my lips!
R. And my mouth will declare your praise!
   Glory be to the Father. . . .

HYMN

READING

So very often we think that we can do very well on our own and forget that we need the help of God our Father. If we are sensible we will be like the son in this story who, although he went off on his own, did come back to His Father.

God our Father will always take us back and give us His great love if we are sensible enough to go back to Him and tell Him we are sorry. The story is in the Good News told by Saint Luke.

And He said, "There was a man who had two sons; and the younger of them said to his father, 'Father, give me the share of property that falls to me.' And he divided his living between them. Not many days later, the younger son gathered all he had and took his journey into a far country, and there he squandered his property in loose living. And when he had spent everything, a great famine arose in that country, and he began to be in want. So he went and joined himself to one of the citizens of that country, who sent him into his fields to feed swine. And he would gladly have fed on the pods that the swine ate; and no one gave him anything. But when he came to himself he said, 'How many of my father's hired servants have bread enough and to spare, but I perish here with hunger! I will arise and go to my father, and I will say to him, Father, I have sinned against heaven and before you; I am no longer worthy to be called your son; treat me as one of your hired servants.' " And he arose and came to his father. But while he was yet at a distance, his father saw him and had compassion, and ran and embraced him and kissed him. And the son said to him, 'Father, I have sinned against heaven and before you; I am no longer worthy to be called your son.' But the father said to his servants, 'Bring quickly the best robe, and put it on him; and put a ring on his hand, and shoes on his feet; and bring the fatted calf and kill it, and let us eat and make merry; for this my son was dead, and is alive again; he was lost, and is found.' And they began to make merry.

PRAYER

Jesus, please help us to know that you are always willing to help us whenever we are in trouble. When we have displeased you, perhaps by saying a lie or by being disobedient, help us to remember the story we have just heard and to know that you will forgive us if we are sorry for our wrong-doing.

V. Lord, hear my prayer!
R. And let my cry come to you.

THE LORD'S PRAYER

BLESSING

Draw near to us, O God, as we lift up our hearts in prayer to you. Bless us and all those who are near and dear to us. Amen.

117. HOW TO PRAY

V. I have lifted up my eyes to the hills!
R. From whence my help comes.
V. My help comes from the Lord!
R. Who made heaven and earth.
   Glory be to the Father. . . .

HYMN

READING

When the Apostles asked our Lord how best to pray He taught them the Lord's Prayer. We should remember this each time we say it. We should try to think what we are really saying. The reading is from the Gospel according to Saint Matthew.

"But when you pray, go into your room and shut the door and pray to your Father who is in secret; and your Father who sees in secret will reward you.

"And in praying do not heap up empty phrases as the Gentiles do; for they think that they will be heard for their many words. Do not be like them, for your Father knows what you need before you ask him. Pray then like this:

"Our Father who art in heaven,
Hallowed be thy name.
Thy kingdom come,
Thy will be done,
   On earth as it is in heaven.
Give us this day our daily bread;
And forgive us our debts,
   As we also have forgiven our debtors;
And lead us not into temptation,
   But deliver us from evil.

"For if you forgive men their trespasses, your heavenly Father also will forgive you; but if you do not forgive men their trespasses, neither will your Father forgive your trespasses."

135

PRAYER

Dear Jesus, bless our school so that working together and playing together, we may learn to love one another and to be more pleasing to you. Help us to praise you and love you for ever. We ask this for your name's sake. Amen.

THE LORD'S PRAYER

BLESSING

Look down with mercy on us as we gather here, O God, and bless all that we do in your name. Through Christ our Lord. Amen.

118. SEE THAT THE LORD IS GOOD!

V. Our help is in the name of the Lord!

R. Who made heaven and earth.

I confess to Almighty God. . . .

HYMN

READING

The reading today is from Psalm 34.

O taste and see that the Lord is good!
Happy is the man who takes refuge in Him!
O fear the Lord, you His saints,
for those who fear Him have no want!
The young lions suffer want and hunger;
but those who seek the Lord lack no good thing.
Come, O sons, listen to me,
I will teach you the fear of the Lord.
What man is there who desires life,
and covets many days, that He may enjoy good?
Keep your tongue from evil,
and your lips from speaking deceit.
Depart from evil, and do good;
seek peace, and pursue it.
The eyes of the Lord are toward the righteous,
and his ears toward their cry.

The face of the Lord is against evildoers,
  to cut off the remembrance of them from the earth.
When the righteous cry for help, the Lord hears,
  and delivers them out of all their troubles.
The Lord is near to the broken-hearted,
  and saves the crushed in spirit.
Many are the afflictions of the righteous;
  but the Lord delivers him out of them all.

PRAYER

We thank you Lord for making the beautiful world and for
keeping us safe during the night. Thank you for all the happiness
you have given us. Help us to make all those happy whom we
meet today. We ask this for the sake of Jesus Christ our Lord.
Amen.

THE LORD'S PRAYER

BLESSING

O God, give us eyes to see all the wonders around us, and hearts
that are always ready to praise you for all your goodness to us,
through Jesus Christ our Lord. Amen.

119. THE ALABASTER BOX OF OINTMENT

V. Praised be Jesus Christ!
R. Praised for evermore!
  Glory be to the Father. . . .

HYMN

READING

Today's reading is from the Good News told by
Saint Luke.

One of the Pharisees asked Him to eat with him,
and He went into the Pharisee's house, and sat at table.
And behold, a woman of the city, who was a sinner,
when she learned that He was sitting at table in the

Pharisee's house, brought an alabaster flask of ointment, and standing behind him at His feet, weeping, she began to wet His feet with her tears, and wiped them with the hair of her head, and kissed His feet, and anointed them with the ointment.

Then turning toward the woman He said to Simon, "Do you see this woman? I entered your house, you gave me no water for my feet, but she has wet my feet with her tears and wiped them with her hair. You gave me no kiss, but from the time I came in she has not ceased to kiss my feet. You did not anoint my head with oil, but she has anointed my feet with ointment. Therefore I tell you, her sins, which are many, are forgiven, for she loved much; but he who is forgiven little, loves little." And He said to her, "Your sins are forgiven." Then those who were at table with Him began to say among themselves, "Who is this, who even forgives sins?" And He said to the woman, "Your faith has saved you; go in peace."

PRAYER

Dear Father in heaven, help us to follow the example of your Son Jesus whom you sent to be an example to us all. Forgive us our sins and bless all that we try to do to please you. Through Jesus Christ our Lord. Amen.

THE LORD'S PRAYER

BLESSING

May your blessing, O Lord, rest on our homes, our parents and our friends and all those we love, both now and evermore. Amen.

120. THE TEMPTATION

V. Blessed be the holy and undivided Trinity!

R. Now and for evermore. Amen.

HYMN

Jesus, who was God, was also truly man, and as man He was tempted just as we are. He shows us how to get rid of temptation by remembering God. The story of His temptation is told by Saint Matthew.

Then Jesus was led up by the Spirit into the wilderness to be tempted by the devil. And He fasted forty days and forty nights, and afterward He was hungry. And the tempter came and said to Him, "If you are the Son of God, command these stones to become loaves of bread." But He answered, "It is written, 'Man shall not live by bread alone, but by every word that proceeds from the mouth of God.' "

Then the devil took Him to the holy city, and set Him on the pinnacle of the temple, and said to Him, "If you are the Son of God, throw yourself down; for it is written, 'He will give His angels charge of you,' and,

'On their hands they will bear you up, lest you strike your foot against a stone.' "

Jesus said to him, "Again it is written, 'You shall not tempt the Lord your God,' " Again, the devil took Him to a very high mountain, and showed Him all the kingdoms of the world and the glory of them; and he said to Him, "All these I will give you, if you will fall down and worship me." Then Jesus said to him, "Begone, Satan! for it is written,

'You shall worship the Lord your God and him only shall you serve.' "

Then the devil left Him, and behold, angels came and ministered to Him.

PRAYER

Dear Jesus, when we are tempted to do anything which is displeasing to you help us to pray and to trust in you to help us. Help us especially when we are with others who want to do wrong. Help us to show them that we should do only those things that are pleasing to you. We ask this for your name's sake. Amen.

V. Lord, hear us!

R. Lord, graciously hear us!

THE LORD'S PRAYER

BLESSING

Help us not be afraid of that which is evil, O Lord, because we
know that you are with us to guide us in all our difficulties. Our
trust is in you, O God, from whom comes all our help. Amen.

121.   ASH WEDNESDAY

We should be careful that the children learn to appreciate that
Jesus suffered once and died for us. He suffers no more for now
He is in glory. During Lent especially, when we are considering
His sufferings and death, it is important to stress this. A help may
be to explain this simply. An aid to understanding may well be to
anticipate Easter and to have a lighted Paschal candle as a sign
of the Risen Christ. Each day a small candle may be solemnly
brought to the Paschal candle and be lit from it. The small candle
would represent our offerings to Jesus.

V. We adore you, O Christ, and we praise you!

R. Because by your Holy Cross you have saved the world!

HYMN

READING

Today is Ash Wednesday and it is the first day of
Lent.

Lent lasts for forty days and reminds us of the forty
days our Lord spent alone in prayer.

In the olden days people who wanted to become
Christians were prepared during Lent, to receive the
Sacrament of Baptism at Easter. Lent was also a time
when sinners did penance so that they would be ready
for the greatest day of the year, which is Easter Day.

140

We are all sinners because we have so often said "No" to God and we have done, or thought, or said things which have displeased Him.

Lent then is a special time when we must all do penance, so that we can be ready for Easter Day.

It is a time when we should think about how well we are trying to live as God's children.

It is a time when we can try to put right some of the things which stop us from being good children of God. For example, most of us are not very good at going to bed when we are told. We like to stay up a little longer perhaps to watch another television programme. And what happens the next day? We are usually tired and bad tempered. And then we do not treat our parents and friends as Jesus wants us to. And then we usually end up by being even sadder. This is one fault that we may have. If it is, then we can try to get rid of it by doing as we are told at bed time.

This is only one fault we may have. Let us think quietly for a moment to see one fault we may have which is keeping us from being good children of God. Let us ask our Lord to help us. Let us decide to try this until the end of the week and see how we have got on. Then we may find out that we shall have to try a little longer or decide to correct some other fault.

(Pause for about half a minute to allow time for thought.)

In Church today, the priest makes a mark on our forehead with blessed ashes. That is why we call today Ash Wednesday. When the ashes are put on us the priest says, "Remember man that you are dust and into dust you will return. . . ." This is to remind us that our soul is more important than our body. It should help us to remember that all that we think or say or do should be done for our Lord.

PRAYER

Help us, O Lord, to pray well and to do penance during the time of Lent, so that we may be more ready to be happy with you on the glorious day of your Resurrection. Through Jesus Christ, your Son, who lives and reigns with you, in the unity of the Holy Spirit, for ever and ever. Amen.

THE LORD'S PRAYER

BLESSING

May the blessing of God, the Father, the Son, and the Holy Spirit, be with us now and always. Amen.

✛

122. JESUS IS CONDEMNED TO DEATH

V. We adore you, O Christ and we praise you!

R. Because by your holy Cross, you have redeemed the world!

HYMN

READING

During Lent we should be trying especially to please God so that we shall be happy with Our Lord on Easter Day. We should be ready for our own Easter Day when we shall be getting ready with our Heavenly Father in His kingdom.

One way of doing this is to think of what our Lord did for us, especially by looking at some of the pictures of the Stations of the Cross, and to think quietly to ourselves about what the picture shows us.

When we look at these pictures we must remember that our Lord suffered in this way but that He is now with His Father, never to suffer any more hurt. But our Lord's sufferings continue in those He suffered and died for. We can offer Him those sufferings. Our Lord lives in each of us by giving us a share of His life and love in the Sacrament of Baptism. Many people imitate Him by accepting their sufferings and sadnesses for Him.

Today as we look at the picture of our Lord condemned to death let us offer Him the sufferings of those who are accused of doing wrong and who are innocent.

Let us ask Him to forgive those who cause suffering by wrongly accusing others.

Jesus, I am sorry for my sins. I will try very hard to love you more.

Let us all stand up and now say a little prayer to ourselves telling Jesus that we are sorry for our sins. Think of a sin you often do and try to think of a way to do better today.

(Pause for about half a minute for a quiet prayer.)

PRAYER

I love you Jesus. I love you more than I can say. I am very sorry for having offended you. Help me never to sin again. Help me to love you always and to be happy with you for ever in heaven. Amen.

THE LORD'S PRAYER

BLESSING

May Jesus who was condemned to death, bless us and help us to love him always. Amen.

Some similar form may be used for each of the Stations.

123. JESUS IS MADE TO CARRY THE CROSS

After He had been condemned to death, Jesus was made to carry a heavy cross up Mount Calvary.

This was a terrible thing for Him to have to do. He had already been whipped and crowned with a crown of thorns. Now He was very weak and through the crowd He tottered and stumbled with this heavy load on His shoulders.

Jesus had done nothing to deserve to suffer. There are many people who suffer and who have done nothing to deserve it. Some people are poor through no fault of their own. They are able to offer their suffering to Christ.

If there is something we need and cannot have, we can offer this suffering or disappointment to our Lord. We should pray too, that we can find a way to help others who suffer. We could perhaps find a way to help a poor person or someone who is lonely.

Say a little prayer to yourselves and think about what you have just heard. Do you know a poor or lonely person you could help?

Tell Jesus that if you are sad or unhappy today you will think of Him.

124. JESUS FALLS THE FIRST TIME

As our Lord staggered and tottered under the weight of the cross, He became weaker and weaker. The rough road made it difficult for Him to keep to His feet. At last He stumbled and fell. The heavy cross fell on top of Him and made Him suffer the more.

Jesus had committed no crime. He had done no sin. All He had ever done was to help us to get closer to God our Father and to show us how to love Him. We often say, "No" to God our Father and are so selfish that we do not really love God. *Pause*

Jesus, I am so ungrateful to you for all you have suffered for me. I am so often selfish and lazy. I will not own up when I have done something wrong. *Pause*

Today we will offer you any aches and pains and sickness that we may have.

Let us all think over in our minds about what we have heard and ask our Lord to help us to be honest and truthful. Let us remember His sufferings for us when He fell under the heavy cross. Let us think of the sufferings of all the sick who offer their sickness and sadness to Him.

125. JESUS MEETS HIS MOTHER

When Jesus was taken from the garden of gethsemane by the soldiers, all His apostles were afraid and ran off. Only Peter followed when He was taken to be wrongly accused. And then Peter left our Lord too.

As He set off on the road to Calvary, all but one of our Lord's friends had left Him. His Mother was there. She saw all His suffering. How sad she was to see Him crowned with thorns and carrying His rough shaped cross on which He was to die! His Mother saw and felt all that He was suffering.

Mary, who was without sin, suffered when she saw our Lord's sufferings.

We offer you today our sorrow for all the worry and sorrow we have caused our mothers by our disobedience, by our answering back, by our selfishness. We will try hard not to make our mothers sad and we will try to make up for all the times we have hurt them.

Let us be quiet for a few moments and think of our Lord's sufferings and the sufferings we have caused our mothers who share the life and love of God.

126. SIMON HELPS TO CARRY THE CROSS

Jesus was getting weaker. The Jews thought that He might die before they had a chance to crucify Him.

There was, amongst the visitors to Jerusalem at that time, a man who had come from North Africa and who was in the crowd along the way to Calvary. The Jews forced this man, Simon from Cyrene, to help our Lord to carry the cross.

Probably, they made fun of Simon and laughed at Him. They said unkind things to him. Perhaps some people thought that Simon was going to be crucified and mocked him too. Simon too, perhaps wondered what would become of him.

But he helped our Lord to carry His cross. How he must have come, in a short time, to love our Lord! Our Lord was not grumbling. He did not answer back when the crowd laughed at Him and said nasty things to Him and about Him. And so, although Simon had been forced to help our Lord, He was soon glad to be helping Him.

I wonder if we love our Lord enough so that we don't mind if our friends make fun of us and laugh at us when we do things to please Him?

Do we do things to please our Lord which, in a way, help us to carry His cross with Him?

Let us ask ourselves how we can help our Lord today and see if we can find one thing to do for him—like not answering back when we feel that we are told off.

Ask our Lord to help you to find just one thing to suffer for Him everyday and like Simon, we will then be helping to carry our Lord's cross.

127. VERONICA WIPES THE FACE OF JESUS

As Jesus made His way up Mount Calvary He became weaker and weaker.

Sweat and blood ran down His face and into His eyes and He could scarcely see His way as He tottered along.

The only act of kindness done to Him was when Veronica offered Him a cloth to wipe His face. This kindness was not an act which needed a lot of bravery. It was a small thing—just a cloth to wipe over His face. And Jesus repaid this act in a wonderful way—He left the mark of His face on the cloth.

Jesus does not ask us to do great and daring deeds. He wants us to do little things often and well. He wants us to do ordinary things which we can see need doing. We need not let anyone know we have done them. We could offer to carry a heavy shopping basket for an old lady. We could go to talk to someone who hasn't many friends or call on some old people to do a message or chop the firewood. Every man, woman and child is someone Jesus came to save. If we think of everyone like that, whatever we do, we do to Jesus and He will never forget the smallest thing we do for His sake.

128. JESUS FALLS THE SECOND TIME

Even though Jesus had help to carry His Cross, it did not mean that His sufferings had finished. He was still weak. He could scarcely see where He was going. His feet were also sore and bleeding. Soon He stumbled and fell again. And this fall hurt Him more than the first. He was tired out and weary, with no one except perhaps Simon to say a kind word to Him. And perhaps Simon was too afraid to speak.

But soon Our Lord was up again to continue His journey. He would not give up.

How often do we promise things to Our Lord! How often do we say that we will do better! And what happens? We try for a little while and then give up. We say, "Oh! It doesn't matter", or, "I'm too tired", or "I can't be bothered". Our Lord did not say things like that. He knew what God our Father wanted Him to do and He did it, no matter what He felt like.

Let us tell Our Lord that no matter how much it hurts us or how little we feel like doing it, we will always do what we know is pleasing to Him. In this way we will be imitating Our Lord.

Think of what you have heard and make up a prayer in your own minds to ask Our Lord to help you never to give up or to give in when things go wrong.

129. THE WOMEN OF JERUSALEM
WEEP FOR JESUS

Not all who were in the crowd along the way of the Cross were haters of Our Lord. We have seen that both Simon and Veronica had helped Him. At one part of the journey Jesus met some of the women from Jerusalem. They were crying bitterly and weeping when they saw His sufferings. They were sorry for Him.

Jesus looked kindly at them and spoke to them. They

were the only words He spoke on the way to Calvary and so they must be very important words and He must want us to think about them.

The words He said to these ladies were, "Do not weep for me but for yourselves and your children."

He was telling them to be sorry for their sins. We should be sorry for our selfishness and lies and all our other sins. Now we are sorry for our sins when we know that they are wrong and we tell God that we are sorry, and that we will try our very best not to do them again. God is so good. He has given us so much.

Let us listen to Him and ask Him to help us never to say "No" to what He wants us to do.

Let us make an act of sorrow together and ask God's grace to keep us in His friendship.

130. JESUS FALLS THE THIRD TIME

I suppose that we often fall down and cut or graze our knees or our hands and arms. And when we do, it can be quite sore. It hurts and it goes on hurting for quite a long time. We cry with the pain.

All this happened to Our Lord as He carried His Cross, but when He fell down His Cross fell on top of Him and made it even worse.

We keep falling in to sin but by the help of God's grace we can get better. If we are truly sorry, then He will forgive us.

No matter how often, or how badly we sin, God will always forgive us if we ask Him. He is always ready to give us grace to help us to keep close to Him. Do we ask for this grace? Do we try to keep close to God? We should often go to Confession to have our sins forgiven and to get the grace we need to keep away from sin.

Tell God now that each evening we will think of anything that we have done during the day which has displeased Him and that we will ask Him to forgive us and to help us to keep close to Him by always doing the things that are pleasing to Him.

131. JESUS REACHES THE PLACE OF CRUCIFIXION

At last the weary, painful journey to the place of Crucifixion is at an end. The Cross is placed on the ground, and Jesus has His clothes torn from His cut and bleeding body. In the midst of the noisy crowd Jesus is silent and prayerful, offering His last and biggest sacrifice to God our Father, for us.

The silence of Our Blessed Lord at this time should be a lesson for us. How much and how often do we suffer in silence for Him? Do we not usually try to make excuses for ourselves, even when we know that we are in the wrong? We are so often dishonest with others when we make excuses and answer back. Let us learn to be silent and truthful and honest. Let us give Him all our thoughts so that we may never think anything we would be ashamed of. When we offer Him our words, we should promise that we will try never to say anything to hurt anyone. And may our offering of our deeds be a promise to do every single thing for the love of Him who offered His every suffering for us.

132. JESUS IS NAILED TO THE CROSS

The cross was on the ground. Jesus was thrown down and His arms were stretched out and His hands nailed to the wood. Then His feet were nailed and the cross lifted up and dropped into a hole in the ground where it stood for all the crowd to see Jesus in His sufferings. He was crucified.

Perhaps this was the worst of all the sufferings of Jesus. He was offering His life to God the Father for us and finishing the offering of the Last Supper. And God the Father accepted the offering.

In every Mass Jesus offers Himself for us and God the Father accepts the offering. When we go to Mass it is like being at the Last Supper and the Crucifixion again.

Jesus offered Himself for us so that we may share His life and His love. Let us thank Him for our Baptism and for Holy Communion and let us offer Him all of our prayers, deeds, sufferings and joys.

133. JESUS DIES ON THE CROSS

For three hours Jesus hung on the Cross. His weight pulled on His nailed hands and feet. His sufferings became worse. On either side of Him hung a thief. A crowd of people stood around laughing at the sufferings of Our Lord and making fun of Him.

At the foot of the cross stood His Mother and with her Saint John and also Mary Magdalene the sinner whose sins had been forgiven because of her love of Our Lord. All His other friends had left Him—afraid of the soldiers who were there and of the angry crowd.

As Our Lord hung there dying, what wonderful words He spoke! He forgave the thief who was sorry for his crimes, He forgave the Jews for crucifying Him, He gave His own Mother to be our Mother.

And just about His last words were, "Into Thy hands, I commit My spirit. It was as though He said, "I have done all I could do. I have done My best. Now Father, I leave everything to you".

What love Our Lord has for each one of us! He gave all—even His life. Let us offer Him all of our life. We will promise to do our best and give our all for Him. If we do that, then nothing matters and we can leave the rest in the hands of God our Father.

134. JESUS IS TAKEN DOWN FROM THE CROSS

After three hours agony Jesus died. His Heart was pierced with a lance. The last drops of blood and water dripped from His side.

Permission was given to take His body from the cross and to prepare it for burial. As Mary had nursed Jesus as a baby, now for the last time she took her Son in her arms and wept.

Mary, Mother of Sorrows, pray for all those who are sad.

Jesus had made His big offering to His Father. God the Father was pleased with His offering and accepted it. Because Jesus did this He rose again and is with His Father in glory.

Dear Mother Mary, help me always to say "Yes" to God. Help me to think for a few moments how I can say "Yes" in a special way today.

135. JESUS IS BURIED

Joseph of Arimethea, a prince, had given His grave to be used as the grave of Our Lord. Quickly Our Lord was got ready for burial and His body placed in the tomb and a great stone rolled over it.

The Jews thought that was the end of Our Lord. So did most other people. Now they could forget all about Him.

But Jesus had said that after three days He would rise again and on Easter Sunday morning, His body, which had been quite dead, He Himself brought back to life. And He rose from the dead.

Jesus, when you rose from the dead, you gave new life to the world. Help all those who do not know you in our own country or in foreign lands to share your life and love so that with you we may all be happy in your kingdom for ever and ever.

136. BEHOLD YOUR SON
—BEHOLD YOUR MOTHER

V. Holy Mary, Mother of God!
R. Pray for us sinners, now and at the hour of our death!

HYMN

READING

Today we are going to start thinking of some of the beautiful words our Lord spoke from the cross.

At the foot of the cross were our Lady and Saint John. Our Lord was of course a good Son and He loved our Blessed Lady very much. Listen to what Saint John tells us.

By the Cross of Jesus were His mother, and His mother's sister and Mary Magdalene. When Jesus saw His mother and the disciple whom He loved standing near, He said to His mother, "Woman, behold your son!" Then He said to the disciple, "Behold your mother!" And from that hour the disciple took her to his own home.

At that moment too Our Lady became the Mother of the Church and our Mother too.

PRAYER

Dear Jesus, when you were dying you gave our Blessed Lady to Saint John to look after and you gave Saint John to our Lady. You have given our Lady to us too to be our Mother. Help us to be good children of our parents so that we may please our Blessed Lady and please you. We will do this best by helping in our own homes and by pleasing our parents. Help us, please. Amen.

THE LORD'S PRAYER

BLESSING

For the sake of your sorrowful Mother, have mercy on us and give us all the blessings we need to be always pleasing to you and to the Father and the Holy Spirit, God, for ever and ever. Amen.

137. FATHER FORGIVE THEM

V. Father, forgive us our trespasses!

R. As we forgive those who trespass against us!

HYMN

READING

When Jesus was dying on the cross and the wicked men were standing around watching Him suffer and die He spoke kindly to them. I wonder if we would have felt kind? We would probably have felt very sorry for ourselves and felt very angry. But Jesus was as kind and generous as He always is. He said, "Father, forgive them." We should always be ready to forgive others. Let us think today if there is anyone who has harmed us in any way. Do we want to be friendly with them? Perhaps we do not speak to them or we say unkind things about them. Let us make up our minds now to forgive them and to be friendly to them. We will think quietly for a few moments about this and see if there is any way in which we can do better.

(Pause for about half a minute.)

PRAYER

Dear Jesus, we always want to be forgiven. Help us to forgive others so that you may forgive us, and we may be always in your friendship. Amen.

THE LORD'S PRAYER

BLESSING

May the blessing of God the Father, Son and Holy Spirit be with us always and forgive us our sins. Amen.

138. THIS DAY YOU SHALL BE WITH ME

V. Lord, Saviour of the weak and heart-broken!

R. Have mercy on us!

HYMN

READING

Two criminals were crucified with our Lord. One was on His right and the other on His left. One of them was not at all sorry for his crimes, and cheekily shouted to our Lord to save Himself and the two who were with Him.

The other began to love God and said that it was quite right that they should be punished for they had done many wrongs. But Jesus, he said, had done no wrong. And he said: "Jesus, remember me when you come in your kingly power." And Jesus said to him, "Truly, I say to you, today you shall be with me in Paradise." Jesus is always ready to take us back into His friendship when we are truly sorry.

PRAYER

Dear Jesus, help me always to love you. Help me always to be sorry for any wrong I ever do. Help me never to be too proud to own up when I have done wrong so that I too, may one day be with you in Paradise.

THE LORD'S PRAYER

BLESSING

May God bless all those who are going to die today and help us always to be pleasing to Him for the sake of Jesus Christ, our Lord. Amen.

139. IT IS FINISHED

V. Into your hands, O Lord,
R. I commend my spirit.

HYMN

READING

Jesus told His apostles that He had come on earth to do the will of His Heavenly Father. All that He ever did, He did to please His Father. He was kind to the poor. He helped the sick. He forgave sins. He even brought some who had died back to life again, to show how good and powerful He was. He did this to show that He had the power to take us to live with Him in His Kingdom after we have died. All this was the work that His Heavenly Father gave Him to do. Many people would not listen to Him and they even put Him to death. Even this He suffered because it was by doing this that He would win for us the life and love of God.

Just before He died, Jesus spoke from the Cross. "It is finished!" He said. He had now completed all that His Father had asked of Him. Now He could return to His Father in glory.

We should always try to do what is pleasing to our Heavenly Father. Then, when it is time for us to be with Jesus in the Heavenly Kingdom, we shall be able to say, "It is finished." We will then know that we have done all that God our Father wants of us. We will be sure that because He is so good, Jesus will then take us to Himself.

PRAYER

Dear Jesus, help us only to do those things which are pleasing to you. We need your help. Do not let us be silly enough to turn away from you to do anything which we know will not please you. Show us what you want us to do and help us to do it for your Name's sake. Amen.

THE LORD'S PRAYER

May the Lord bless us and keep us. May the light of his countenance shine on us and give us His peace. Amen.

140. JESUS WASHES THE FEET OF THE DISCIPLES

V. A new law I give you!

R. That you love one another!

HYMN

READING

Before Jesus had His Last Supper with the Apostles everything had to be got ready. In Israel the roads were always dusty and it was polite to give the guests water to wash their hands and feet. Perhaps if you were important enough to have a servant he would wash the feet of the guests.

Our Lord, poured water into a basin and began to wash the disciples' feet and to wipe them with the towel with which He was girded. . . . When He had washed their feet, and taken His garments and resumed His place, He said to them: "Do you know what I have done to you? You call me Teacher and Lord; and you are right, for so I am. If I then your Teacher and Lord have washed your feet . . . you also ought to wash one another's feet. For I have given you an example, that you should also do as I have done to you. . . . Truly, truly, I say to you, he who receives anyone whom I send, receives me. . . . A new commandment I give you that you love one another. By this all men will know that you are my disciples, if you have love for one another."

Our Lord, who was God, washed His disciples' feet. He was not too proud to be like a servant to show how much He loved us and would do for us. He tells us that we must help other people. It is Christian to love and help others. If we do not love and help others we cannot love God. This is the new commandment He gave to us. We cannot love God if we do not love our neighbour. How can we be too proud to bother with others? How can we quarrel or say unkind things about others, or not speak to others? We must love others as Jesus loves us.

PRAYER

Dear Jesus, you taught us so well and we so very often show that we have not learned the lesson you came to teach us. Help us to be cheerful and kind to everybody, especially those who have no friends. Help us never to say or do any unkind thing because if we do it will be like doing it to you. You said, "If you do it to one of these little ones, you do it to me." Help us now, just before Easter, to try extra hard to think of other people and to make up our minds never to be unkind or unfriendly.

THE LORD'S PRAYER

BLESSING

May the God of love pour into our hearts and minds a love of others for the sake of Jesus Christ our Lord. Amen.

141. THE LAST SUPPER

V. O Sacrament most holy, O Sacrament Divine!

R. All praise and all thanksgiving be every moment thine.

HYMN

READING

For the last few days of Lent we will listen to some of the story of Our Lord's last days on earth, as it is written in the Good News. Today the reading is from Saint Paul's first letter to the people of Corinth.

For I received from the Lord what I also delivered to you, that the Lord Jesus on the night when he was

157

betrayed took bread, and when He had given thanks, He broke it, and said, "This is my body which is for you. Do this in remembrance of me." In the same way also the cup, after supper, saying, "This cup is the new covenant in my blood. Do this, as often as you drink it, in remembrance of me." For as often as you eat this bread and drink the cup, you proclaim the Lord's death until He comes.

PRAYER

Jesus, I thank you for the great Sacrament of Holy Communion. Whenever I receive you please help me to remember that you suffered for me and that you left me this great Sacrament to be the special way of making sure I always remember you love me. Help me as I kneel with others to receive you to remember to love them for your sake. Amen.

THE LORD'S PRAYER

BLESSING

May we receive all your graces and blessings, Lord, from the most Holy Sacrament of Communion.

142. THE ARREST

V. O God, come to my assistance!
R. Lord, make haste to help me!
    I Confess. . . .

HYMN

READING

The reading today is from the Good News told by Saint Mark.

And they went to a place which was called Gethsemane; and He said to His disciples, "Sit here, while I pray." And He took with Him Peter and James and John, and began to be greatly distressed and troubled. And He said to them, "My soul is very sorrowful, even to death; remain here and watch."

And He came and found them sleeping, and He said to Peter, "Simon, are you asleep? Could you not watch one hour?"

And immediately, while He was still speaking, Judas came, one of the twelve, and with Him a crowd with swords and clubs from the chief priests and the scribes and the elders. Now the betrayer had given them a sign, saying, "The one I shall kiss is the man; seize him and lead him away safely." And when he came, he went up to Him at once, and said, "Master!" And he kissed Him. And they laid hands on Him and seized Him. But one of those who stood by drew his sword, and struck the slave of the high priest and cut off his ear. And Jesus said to them, "Have you come out as against a robber, with swords and clubs to capture me? Day after day I was with you in the temple teaching, and you did not seize me. But let the scriptures be fulfilled." And they all forsook Him, and fled.

PRAYER

Jesus, you came to teach us all by your example. When wicked men treated you cruelly you suffered for our sakes. Help us never to offend you and to show that we love you by following your example and by loving our neighbours as ourselves. Amen.

THE LORD'S PRAYER

BLESSING

May the grace of our Lord Jesus Christ and the love of God and the fellowship of the Holy Spirit be with us all evermore. Amen.

143. PETER'S DENIAL

V. O Lord, open my lips!

R. And my mouth shall declare your praise.

Glory be to the Father. . . .

HYMN

READING

Peter said that he would never deny that he knew our Lord. He did not want to but he thought that he was strong enough himself. When he found out how wrong he was, he was sorry and never again forgot that he could do nothing without the help of God's grace.

The reading today is from the Good News told by Saint John and Saint Luke.

Simon Peter followed Jesus, and so did another disciple. As this disciple was known to the high priest, he entered the court of the high priest along with Jesus, while Peter stood outside at the door. So the other disciple, who was known to the high priest, went out and spoke to the maid who kept the door, and brought Peter in. The maid who kept the door said to Peter, "Are not you also one of this man's disciples?" He said, "I am not." And when they had kindled a fire in the middle of the courtyard and sat down together, Peter sat among them. Then a maid, seeing him as he sat in the light and gazing at him, said, "This man also was with him." But he denied it, saying, "Woman, I do not know him." And a little later some one else saw him and said "You also are one of them." But Peter said, "Man, I am not." And after an interval of about an hour still another insisted, saying, "Certainly this man also was with him; for he is a Galilean." But Peter said, "Man, I do not know what you are saying." And immediately, while he was still speaking, the cock crowed. And the Lord turned and looked at Peter. And Peter remembered the word of the Lord, how He had said to him, "Before the cock crows today, you will deny me three times." And he went out and wept bitterly.

PRAYER

Jesus, you must have been very sad when all your friends left you. Help us never to let you down by saying that we are Christians and then not living as Christians. Give us the courage to stand up for you and your ways. Send your Holy Spirit to give us courage and to make us strong. Encourage us by your presence among us as we pray the words you taught us to pray. . . . Our Father. . . .

BLESSING

Receive our prayers, O God, when we call on you and give us your peace all the days of our life, through Jesus Christ our Lord. Amen.

144. THE TRIAL BEFORE PILATE

V. I have lifted up my eyes to the hills!
R. From whence my help comes.
V. My help comes from the Lord!
R. Who made heaven and earth.
    Glory be to the Father. . . .

HYMN

READING

The reading today is from the Gospel according to Saint Luke.

Pilate then called together the chief priests and the rulers and the people, and said to them, "You brought me this man as one who was perverting the people; and after examining him before you, behold, I did not find this man guilty of any of your charges against him; neither did Herod, for he sent him back to us. Behold, nothing deserving death has been done by him; I will therefore chastise him and release him."

But they all cried out together, "Away with this man, and release to us Barabbas"—a man who had been thrown into prison for an insurrection started in the city, and for murder. Pilate addressed them once more, desiring to release Jesus; but they shouted out, "Crucify, crucify him!" A third time he said to them, "Why, what evil has he done? I have found in him no crime deserving death; I will therefore chastise Him and release Him." But they were urgent, demanding with loud cries that He should be crucified. And their voices prevailed. So Pilate gave sentence that their demand should be granted. He released the man who had been thrown into prison for insurrection and murder, whom they asked for; but Jesus He delivered up to their will.

PRAYER

O Lord, our God, who sent your son, our Saviour Christ our Lord to suffer for our sakes, grant that we may all follow His great example of humility and patience so that we may enjoy the grace of the Resurrection. Through Jesus Christ our Lord. Amen.

THE LORD'S PRAYER

BLESSING

May God grant to us the knowledge of what He wants of us and give us the happiness which comes of doing His Will. Amen.

145. THE CRUCIFIXION

V. We adore you, O Christ, and we praise you!
R. Because by your Holy Cross you have redeemed the world.

HYMN

READING

The reading is from the Good News told by Saint Mark.

And the soldiers led him away inside the palace (that is, the praetorium); and they called together the whole battalion. And they clothed him in a purple cloak, and plaiting a crown of thorns they put it on Him. And they began to salute Him, "Hail, King of the Jews!" And they struck His head with a reed, and spat upon Him, and they knelt down in homage to Him. And when they had mocked Him, they stripped Him of the purple cloak, and put His own clothes on Him. And they led Him out to crucify Him.

And they compelled a passer-by, Simon of Cyrene, who was coming in from the country, the father of Alexander and Rufus, to carry His cross. And they brought Him to the place called Golgotha (which means the place of a skull). And they offered Him wine mingled with myrrh; but He did not take it. And they crucified Him, and divided His garments among them, casting lots for them, to decide what each should take. And it was the third hour, when they crucified Him. And the inscription of the charge against Him read, "The King of the Jews."

PRAYER

V. Jesus, You came on earth to free us from our sins.

R. We give you thanks, Lord Jesus!

V. Because you faced your persecutors even though you had done no wrong,

R. We thank you, Lord Jesus!

V. Because, when all left you, you went on to the end, upheld by our Father in heaven,

R. We thank you, Lord Jesus.

V. Because you had a special place in your heart for children and told them to come to you,

R. We thank you, Lord Jesus!

V. Because you pardoned all those who wronged you,

R. We thank you, Lord Jesus!
   Lamb of God, who takes on Himself the sins of the world, have mercy on us!

146. THE RESURRECTION

V. O Queen of heaven rejoice. Alleluia!

R. For He whom Thou didst merit to bear, Alleluia!

V. Has risen as He said, Alleluia!

R. Pray for us, to God, Alleluia!

HYMN

READING

The reading is from the Good News told by Saint Mark.

And when the sabbath was past, Mary Magdalene, and Mary the mother of James, and Salome, bought spices, so that they might go and anoint him. And very early on the first day of the week they went to the tomb when the sun had risen. And they were saying to one another, "Who will roll away the stone for us from the door of the tomb?" And looking up, they saw that the stone was rolled back; for it was very large. And entering the tomb, they saw a young man sitting on the right side, dressed in a white robe; and they were amazed. And he said to them, "Do not be amazed; you seek Jesus of Nazareth, who was crucified. He has risen, he is not here; see the place where they laid Him. But go, tell His disciples and Peter that He is going before you to Galilee; there you will see Him, as He told you."

PRAYER

O Lord, who on Easter day conquered death and opened the gates of heaven, help us to have a great longing for heaven so that we may be with you for ever and ever. Amen.

THE LORD'S PRAYER

BLESSING

May the blessing of the risen Lord fill our hearts with joy and obtain for us every good gift today and always. Amen.

147. THE ROAD TO EMMAUS

V. The Lord has risen, indeed.

R. Alleluia!

HYMN

READING

On the evening of Easter day, our glorified Lord appeared to some disciples who were on their way back from Jerusalem to Emmaus. They were talking about all that had happened to Jesus. They said what a wonderful person He had been. They thought that He was the Saviour promised by God but that now He had been crucified. Jesus spoke with them and explained many things to them about the kingdom of God. They did not realise who this stranger was who was walking with them. When He was about to go they asked Him to stay with them for a little while and He went in to have a meal with them. Saint Luke says, "When He was at table, with them, He took bread and blessed, and broke it, and gave it to them. And their eyes were opened and they recognised Him; and he vanished out of their sight. . . . And they rose that same hour and returned to Jerusalem; and they found the eleven gathered together and those who were with them, who said. "The Lord has risen indeed, and has appeared to Simon!" Then they told what had happened on the road, and how He was known to them in the breaking of bread.

PRAYER

O Lord Jesus, who by the Easter festival has given medicine to a sick world, we pray you to give your people gifts from heaven so that they may obtain perfect freedom and move onwards to eternal life; through our Lord Jesus Christ your Son, who lives and reigns with you and the Holy Spirit, world without end. Amen.

THE LORD'S PRAYER

165

148. JESUS APPEARS TO THE APOSTLES

V. O God, come to my assistance!
R. O Lord, make haste to help me.
Glory be to the Father. . . .

HYMN

READING

The reading is from the Good News told by Saint Luke.

Jesus himself stood among them, and said to them, "Peace to you!" But they were startled and frightened, and supposed that they saw a spirit. And He said to them, "Why are you troubled, and why do questionings rise in your hearts? See my hands and my feet, that it is I myself; handle me, and see; for a spirit has not flesh and bones as you see that I have." And when He had said this, He showed them His hands and His feet. And while they still disbelieved for joy, and wondered, He said to them, "Have you anything here to eat?" They gave him a piece of broiled fish, and He took it and ate before them.

Then He said to them, "These are my words which I spoke to you, while I was still with you, that everything written about me in the law of Moses and the prophets and the psalms must be fulfilled." Then He opened their minds to understand the scriptures.

PRAYER

O God, grant that we may always be true to the promises we made in the Sacrament of Baptism so that we may love and serve you more and more, through Jesus Christ our risen Lord. Amen.

BLESSING

May our risen Lord fill us with faith, hope and the love of God, and our neighbour, all the days of our lives. Amen.

149. JESUS BY THE LAKE

V. Alleluia! Alleluia!
R. The Lord has risen indeed! Alleluia.

HYMN

READING

The reading today tells of how our Lord, risen from the dead, showed Himself to the disciples for the third time. Saint John tells us of this in his Good News.

After this Jesus revealed Himself again to the disciples by the Sea of Tiberias; and He revealed himself in this way. Simon Peter, Thomas called the Twin, Nathanael of Cana in Galilee, the sons of Zebedee, and two others of His disciples were together. Simon Peter said to them, "I am going fishing." They said to him, "We will go with you." They went out and got into the boat; but that night they caught nothing.

Just as day was breaking, Jesus stood on the beach; yet the disciples did not know that it was Jesus. Jesus said to them, "Children, have you any fish?" They answered him, "No." He said to them, "Cast the net on the right side of the boat, and you will find some." So they cast it, and now they were not able to haul it in, for the quantity of fish. That disciple whom Jesus loved said to Peter, "It is the Lord!" When Simon Peter heard that it was the Lord, he put on his clothes, for he was stripped for work, and sprang into the sea. But the other disciples came in the boat, dragging the net full of fish, for they were not far from the land but about a hundred yards off.

When they got out on land, they saw a charcoal fire there, with fish lying on it, and bread. Jesus said to them, "Bring some of the fish that you have just caught." So Simon Peter went aboard and hauled the net ashore, full of large fish, a hundred and fifty-three of them; and although there were so many, the net was not torn. Jesus said to them, "Come and have breakfast." Now none of the disciples dared ask Him, "Who are you?" They knew it was the Lord. Jesus came and took the bread and gave it to them, and so with the fish. This was now the third time that Jesus was revealed to the disciples after He was raised from the dead.

PRAYER

O God, you give us this great feast of Easter every year. Grant that the way we keep this feast in this life will help us to obtain joy in your everlasting kingdom. Through our Lord, Jesus Christ, who lives and reigns with you, and the Holy Spirit, one God, world without end. Amen.

THE LORD'S PRAYER

BLESSING

May the risen Lord fill our hearts with all the graces and blessings we need. Amen.

150.   JESUS AND MARY MAGDALENE

V. Alleluia! Alleluia!
R. The Lord has risen indeed! Alleluia!

HYMN

READING

The reading today tells how our Lord appeared to Mary Magdalene. It is from the Good News told by Saint John.

But Mary stood weeping outside the tomb, and as she wept she stooped to look into the tomb; and she saw two angels in white, sitting where the body of Jesus had lain, one at the head and one at the feet. They said to her, "Woman, why are you weeping?" She said to them, "Because they have taken away my Lord and I do not know where they have laid Him." Saying this, she turned round and saw Jesus standing, but she did not know that it was Jesus. Jesus said to her, "Woman, why are you weeping? Whom do you seek?" Supposing him to be the gardener, she said to him, "Sir, if you have carried Him away tell me where you have laid Him, and I will take Him away." Jesus said to her, "Mary." She turned and said to him in Hebrew. "Rabboni!" (which means, Teacher). Jesus said to her, "Do not hold me, for I have not yet ascended to the Father; but go to my brethren and say to them, I am ascending to my Father and your Father, to my God and your God." Mary Magdalene went and said to the disciples, "I have seen the Lord"; and she told them that He had said these things to her.

PRAYER

O Lord, you have given to so many a share in the life of God, grant that all who have been born again in the waters of Baptism may be one in faith and good deeds. Through Jesus Christ our Lord. Amen.

THE LORD'S PRAYER

BLESSING

May the blessing of the risen Lord fill our hearts and minds with His life and love. Through Christ our Lord. Amen.

151. PETER AND JOHN AT THE TOMB

V. Alleluia! Alleluia!
R. The Lord is risen indeed! Alleluia!

HYMN

READING

The reading today is from the Good News told by Saint John.

Now on the first day of the week Mary Magdalene came to the tomb early, while it was still dark, and saw that the stone had been taken away from the tomb. So she ran, and went to Simon Peter and the other disciple, the one whom Jesus loved, and said to them, "They have taken the Lord out of the tomb and we do not know where they have laid Him." Peter then came out with the other disciple, and they went toward the tomb. They both ran, but the other disciple outran Peter and reached the tomb first; and stooping to look in, he saw the linen cloths lying there, but he did not go in. Then Simon Peter came, following him, and went into the tomb; he saw the linen cloths lying, and the napkin, which had been on His head, not lying with the linen cloths, but rolled up in a place by itself. Then the other disciple, who reached the tomb first, also went in, and he saw and believed.

PRAYER

Grant we pray you, Almighty God, that we who have celebrated Easter may be able, by taking part in its celebration, reverently, to have unending joy in your heavenly kingdom. Through Christ our Lord. Amen.

THE LORD'S PRAYER

BLESSING

May all the blessings of our risen Lord join us to Him for ever more. Amen.

152. THE MISSION OF THE APOSTLES

V. Send forth your Spirit and they will be created!
R. And you will renew the face of the earth!
Glory be to the Father. . . .

HYMN

READING

Today Saint Matthew tells us of the work Jesus gave to His apostles.

Now the eleven disciples went to Galilee, to the mountain to which Jesus had directed them. And when they saw Him they worshipped Him; but some doubted. And Jesus came and said to them, "All authority in heaven and on earth has been given to me. Go therefore and make disciples of all nations, baptizing them in the name of the Father and of the Son and of the Holy Spirit, teaching them to observe all that I have commanded you; and lo, I am with you always, to the close of the age."

PRAYER

Dear Jesus, at Easter time you made us able to be at one with our Heavenly Father once more. Send your Holy Spirit into our hearts so that we may be able to keep our promise to you. Through Jesus Christ our Lord. Amen.

THE LORD'S PRAYER

BLESSING

May the blessing of God, the Father, the Son, and the Holy Spirit be with us now and always. Amen.

153. THE GOOD SHEPHERD

V. Lord, open my lips!

R. And my mouth shall declare your praise.

Glory be to the Father. . . .

HYMN

READING

A shepherd's job is to look after sheep. It is a hard job and a lonely one. There is a lot of work to be done, especially at this time of year when there are so many lambs about.

Sheep are silly animals. They wander off. They get caught in briars. They climb down dangerous paths and get into difficulties and can't get back unless the shepherd has kept his eye on them and finds them and saves them.

A good shepherd knows his sheep. He follows after them; he protects them; he often has to stay up all night with them, especially at lambing time.

We are very much like sheep. We are often stupid. We wander from the way God wants us to go. Like sheep which get caught by briars we get caught by our sins. We do things which are dangerous to our souls like being disobedient, dishonest or untruthful. We miss or forget our prayers. And yet we are not like sheep because we can all think and choose. And so we are, in a way, more stupid than sheep because we choose to do these silly things.

Like sheep we need a shepherd to look after us. Our shepherd is our Lord. He tells us in the Gospel, "I am the good shepherd. I know my own and my own know me, as the Father knows me and I know the Father."

Our Lord, like a good shepherd, is always watching over us. He is always ready to help us no matter how much trouble we give Him. If we offend Him by being proud or disobedient or selfish or unkind, He will always forgive us if we are sorry. He will keep us from all dangers if we will only listen to what He has to say to us.

> Loving Shepherd of Thy sheep,
> Keep me Lord, in safety, keep.
> Nothing can Thy power withstand,
> None can pluck me from Thy hand.

PRAYER

O loving Shepherd, who gave your life on the Cross so that we may live, give us gladness so that we whom you have rescued from all

172

dangers may at last come to enjoy everlasting happiness with you in heaven. Who with the Father and the Holy Spirit, live and reign, one God, world without end. Amen.

THE LORD'S PRAYER

BLESSING

May the Lord bless us and keep us. May the light of His countenance shine on us and give us His peace. Amen.

154. OUR BLESSED LADY

V. Hail Mary! Full of grace. The Lord is with thee!
R. Blessed art thou among women and blessed is the fruit of thy womb, Jesus!

HYMN

READING

May is the month of our Blessed Lady and during this month we should think of her often and say a lot of prayers to her and bring her presents of flowers to put near her statue.

Our Lady is the mother of God. She is our mother too. At home, if we are in trouble we always run to mother to tell her of our troubles. We share lots of secrets with her. If we are happy or excited about anything we tell her. If we want anything we usually ask her first.

Mary is an even better mother than our mother at home, and we all know how much she does for us. We should talk to Mary often—tell her our troubles, our secrets, our happiness, our wants. Mary can get for us all the graces we need. Our Lord will refuse her nothing that is good for us.

We should ask her especially for the grace to do what God wants us to do. When the angel Gabriel brought God's message that He wanted her to be the

173

Mother of His Son, Mary knew that she was not fit for such an honour, but because God wanted it she answered, "Behold the handmaid of the Lord. Let it be done unto me according to Thy word."

Our Lord, as a man, in the agony in the garden, felt that He could not bear the sufferings He was to have, but He said to His Father, "Not my will, but thine be done."

Let us ask our Lady to get the grace for us always to do what God wants us to do and not to worry about what we want to do.

PRAYER

O Lord, bless our school, that working together and playing together, we may learn to love one another and to serve you. May our Blessed Lady, Mother of God, watch over us and carry our prayers to her Son. Jesus, Mary and Joseph, I give you my heart and my soul.

THE LORD'S PRAYER

BLESSING

May the blessing of God Almighty, the Father, Son, and Holy Spirit, come to us and remain with us always. Amen.

155. THE ENGLISH MARTYRS

V. Blessed be the Holy and Undivided Trinity!
R. Now and for evermore. Amen.

HYMN

READING

Today is the feast of the English Martyrs.

A martyr is someone who has died rather than give up his faith.

About four hundred years ago the church in England had many enemies. These enemies of the church did not want to do all the things God wanted of them. They had forgotten our Lady's prayer, "Let it be unto me according to Thy word." They were selfish and sinful and cruel to those who wanted to be faithful to God. They put many of them to death. These holy people who died rather than displease God, were martyrs. They had a strong faith and a great love of God and our Blessed Lady. They wanted to love God rather than to please men who were the enemies of God. They were put in prison, tortured and died cruel deaths. Some of them were important people like Saint Thomas More who was the King's best friend. He loved God and the church even more than his king. Saint John Fisher was an important Bishop who was put to death. There were priests like Blessed Edmund Campion; there were school teachers like Blessed Richard Gwyn and many holy women like Blessed Margaret Clitherow and Blessed Ann Lyne.

Today we should think of these English martyrs and ask them to pray that our faith may always be strong, and that we should have a great love of God. We should ask them to pray for our country that more people will learn to love God.

All our English martyrs were great and holy people. We should try to find out more about them so that we can learn from them how to love God more and more.

PRAYER

O God, who from the beginning of our English Church gave us a great love of our Blessed Lady and made us loving subjects of Saint Peter, prince of the Apostles, give us the grace through them to love you more and more. Amen.

THE LORD'S PRAYER

BLESSING

Bless us O Lord with a sure faith and give us a great love for you. Amen.

156. THE FEAST OF SAINTS PHILIP AND JAMES

V. Our help is in the name of the Lord!

R. Who made heaven and earth!

Glory be to the Father. . . .

HYMN

READING

Our Lord chose as His special friends twelve men whom we call the Apostles. These men had special teaching from Our Lord to get them ready for the work He asked them to do. On the first Holy Thursday He made them His first priests and bishops. To them He gave the power to change bread and wine into His own Body and Blood. He gave them the power to forgive sins. Just before He ascended to heaven after His Resurrection, He gave them a special message. "Go," He said to them, "and teach all nations and baptise them in the name of the Father and of the Son and of the Holy Spirit."

Today is the feast day of two of the Apostles, Saints Philip and James. They both became missioners and went to teach others about our Lord. Saint Philip went to Turkey and preached our Lord's message. There he was stoned and then crucified.

Saint James was a cousin of our Lord. He was privileged to be with our Lord when He brought the little daughter of Jairus to life. He went up the mountain with our Lord when He was transfigured and was with Him in the Garden when He was in agony before the Crucifixion. He wrote an Epistle specially for the Jewish people. In it he tells us to be careful how we speak. We should always be kind and charitable when we speak about anyone. Even if we are talking about someone we do not like we should always find something good to say about them.

176

Like the other apostles, Saint James was a martyr. He was taken to the highest part of the Temple in Jerusalem—the very spot where our Lord had been tempted by the devil—and from there he was thrown to death.

We should pray to the apostles for all missionary priests and nuns for help in their work in spreading the teaching of our Lord, and also for the gift of a strong faith for ourselves.

PRAYER

O God, who makes us so happy on this feast day of the holy apostles and martyrs, Saints Philip and James, give us the grace to learn from their good example. Through Christ our Lord. Amen.

THE LORD'S PRAYER

BLESSING

May the Lord bless us and keep us. May the light of His countenance shine on us and give us His grace. Amen.

157. SAINT AUGUSTINE

V. Praised be Jesus Christ!
R. Praised for evermore.

HYMN

READING

Well over a thousand years ago when the Romans ruled our country, some young children were taken to Rome to be sold as slaves. Pope Gregory was walking through the streets of Rome and saw them and asked who they were. He was told that they were Angles for the part of the country they were from was then called Angle land. Pope Gregory said that they looked more like Angels and was very sad when he learned that they did not know anything about our Lord.

So Gregory looked for a good and holy man to send to England to teach the English about our Lord, and to help the English to be Christians. He chose a man called Augustine to make the long journey to England on foot and by boat. Augustine brought with him a group of monks and the King gave permission for them to build a monastery in Canterbury.

There Augustine and his monks worked and prayed and soon many people, when they saw the good and holy lives Augustine and his monks were leading, became their friends. Many asked if they could be baptised and become Christians. Before long the King and most of the people became Christians and tried their best to be pleasing to God. Augustine was made the first Archbishop of Canterbury, and England started to become a Christian country. We should thank God for His goodness in sending Saint Augustine to us so long ago and for the example he showed to the people who then wanted to be like him and to learn to love our Lord.

PRAYER

O God, who gave the gift of faith to the English people through the preaching and miracles of Saint Augustine, grant that by His prayers England may once again be Catholic and that we may always do your will, through Christ our Lord. Amen.

THE LORD'S PRAYER

BLESSING

Look down on us in mercy as we gather here, O God, and bless all that we do in your name, through Christ our Lord. Amen.

158. ROGATION DAYS

V. Our help is in the name of the Lord!
R. Who made heaven and earth.
I confess to Almighty God. . . .

HYMN

READING

Monday, Tuesday and Wednesday before the feast of the Ascension of our Lord into heaven are called Rogation days.

Rogation days are special 'asking' days. They are days on which we specially ask Almighty God to bless the crops that are growing and our factories and mines and to give us all the good things that we need.

Before the Mass on the first day there is a procession outside church. In the olden days it used to go all round the parish. During the procession, the Litany of the Saints is sung and special prayers are said.

In this way the church reminds us how important prayer is. We need to pray often for everyone and everything that we need for all good things come from God. Perhaps today we should think especially of those who have not enough food to keep them healthy and also pray that there may be many more priests to teach all people to come to know and love God and to receive Him in Holy Communion.

PRAYER

We trust you, O God, to hear our prayer for all the things we need. Protect us always and help us when we are in trouble. Through our Lord Jesus Christ your Son, who lives and reigns with you and the Holy Spirit, one God world without end. Amen.

159. THE SECOND ROGATION DAY

V. O Lord, open my lips!
R. And my mouth will declare your praise.
   Glory be to the Father. . . .

HYMN

READING

The reading today is from the Epistle of Saint James.

Therefore confess your sins to one another, and pray for one another, that you may be healed. The prayer of a righteous man has great power in its effects. Elijah was a man of like nature with ourselves and he prayed fervently that it might not rain, and for three years and six months it did not rain on the earth. Then he prayed again and the heaven gave rain, and the earth brought forth its fruit.

My brethren, if any one among you wanders from the truth and some one brings him back, let him know that whoever brings back a sinner from the error of his way will save his soul from death and will cover a multitude of sins.

PRAYER

Grant, O Lord, that we who rely on you to help us in all our troubles may be strengthened against all our temptations by your unceasing protection. Through Christ our Lord. Amen.

THE LORD'S PRAYER

BLESSING

May God bless us and all that we think, or say or do this day and always. Amen.

160. THE THIRD ROGATION DAY

V. I have lifted up my eyes to the hills!
R. From whence my help comes.
V. My help comes from the Lord.
R. Who made heaven and earth.
Glory be to the Father. . . .

HYMN

READING

When Christ ascended into heaven after His Resurrection He went to prepare a place for us with His Father. He took with Him all those who had been waiting for Him, to make all men at one with God again. He has gifts for all of us. Some He wants to be priests and missioners, some He wants to be teachers or doctors, or housewives, or to work in factories and offices. These jobs He wants us to do so that we can live good Christian lives and show all the people we are with how we love God. In this way all will be getting ready to share in the kingdom He has prepared for us. We should then do all the things as well as we can, for all that we think or say or do should be for the honour and glory of God. We ought not to think that what we do is not important. God has chosen us by sharing His life and love with us so that all together we may praise Him and love Him for ever in His Kingdom. There we shall never more be troubled or worried or unhappy or sad but we will have never ending joy and happiness.

PRAYER

O God, from whom all good things come, we pray you to help us always to think right thoughts and by your guidance to put them into practice. Through Christ our Lord. Amen.

THE LORD'S PRAYER

BLESSING

May God bless us and all His people and keep us in His love, now and always. Amen.

161. FRIDAY AFTER THE ASCENSION

V. Come Holy Spirit, fill the hearts of your faithful and kindle in them the fire of your love. Send forth your Spirit and they shall be created.

R. And you will renew the face of the earth.

HYMN

READING

Before our Lord ascended into heaven, He told His apostles that He would not leave them alone like orphans, but that He would send the Holy Spirit to look after them and His Church.

The Holy Spirit was to confirm or make strong the faith of the apostles so that they would be fearless in doing what God wanted of them.

After the Ascension, the apostles were afraid and went back to Jerusalem and locked themselves in the upper room with Our Lady. There they waited and prayed for the coming of the Holy Spirit.

During the time between the Ascension and Pentecost, we should be praying hard that the Holy Spirit will make our faith strong. He will make sure that we have all the graces we need when things are hard for us and we are tempted to sin. When we are not sure what God would like us to do, we should pray to the Holy Spirit and He will give us the grace to know God's will for us.

We must be ready to receive His grace. If our parents put our meals on the table and we never eat anything, we will get hungry, thin, sick and at last, if we continue to refuse food, we shall die.

We will only receive the graces and gifts of the Holy Spirit if we take them. We take or receive God's graces especially by saying our prayers every day, by hearing Holy Mass and by receiving Holy Communion often.

Come, Holy Spirit, and fill our hearts with the fire of Your love.

PRAYER

Almighty God, make our wills always devoted to you. May our hearts be filled with your Holy Spirit so that we may always be pleasing to you, through Christ our Lord. Amen.

THE LORD'S PRAYER

BLESSING

May God the Father, God the Son, and God the Holy Spirit, bless us and keep us now and always. Amen.

182

162. NAAMAN THE SYRIAN

V. O God, come to my assistance!

R. Lord, make haste to help me.

Glory be to the Father. . . .

HYMN

READING

The reading today is from the second book of
Kings.

Naaman, commander of the army of the king of
Syria, was a great man with his master and in high
favour, because by him the Lord had given victory to
Syria. He was a mighty man of valour, but he was a
leper. Now the Syrians on one of their raids had carried
off a little maid from the land of Israel, and she waited
on Naaman's wife. She said to her mistress, "Would
that my lord were with the prophet who is in Samaria!
He would cure him of his leprosy." So Naaman went in
and told his lord, "Thus and so spoke the maiden from
the land of Israel." And the king of Syria said, "Go
now, and I will send a letter to the king of Israel."
So he went, taking with him ten talents of silver,
six thousand shekels of gold, and ten festal garments.
And he brought the letter to the king of Israel, which
read, "When this letter reaches you, know that I have
sent to you Naaman my servant, that you may cure him
of his leprosy." So Naaman came with his horses and
chariots, and halted at the door of Elisha's house. And
Elisha sent a messenger to him, saying, "Go and wash
in the Jordan seven times, and your flesh shall be
restored, and you shall be clean." But Naaman was
angry, and went away, saying, "Behold, I thought that
he would surely come out to me, and stand, and call
on the name of the Lord his God and wave his hand
over the place, and cure the leper. Are not Abana and
Pharpar, the rivers of Damascus, better than all the

183

waters of Israel? Could I not wash in them, and be clean?" So he turned and went away in a rage. But his servants came near and said to him, "My father, if the prophet had commanded you to do some great thing, would you not have done it? How much rather, then, when he says to you, 'Wash, and be clean'?" So he went down and dipped himself seven times in the Jordan, according to the word of the man of God; and his flesh was restored like the flesh of a little child, and he was clean.

PRAYER

O Lord, you healed Naaman's leprosy by the cleansing waters of the river, please cleanse us from all that displeases you. Help us always to listen to those whom you send to teach us what you want from us. Through Christ our Lord. Amen.

THE LORD'S PRAYER

BLESSING

And now to God the Father, God the Son, and God the Holy Spirit, be praise and glory for ever. Amen.

163. THE FEAST OF THE SACRED HEART

V. Most Sacred Heart of Jesus!
R. We put all our trust in you.

HYMN

READING

On this feast day of the Sacred Heart we should think of our Lord's great love for us in coming on earth and in suffering and dying for us. The greatest sign of friendship is that we should be ready to do anything to help our friends and if needs be, even to die for them. Our Lord did this for us. When He was on the cross and had died a soldier stabbed His heart with a spear.

184

Our Lord's heart was really broken for love of us. We should love Him in return. It is hard to love someone and to do things for them if they do not love you back. We shall show the Sacred Heart of Jesus that we love Him if we are willing to do things for Him. We should do some special acts of love to make up to Him for all the times we have not loved Him enough, and to make up for all the sins committed by many wicked people who know Him and hate Him in spite of His love and who do many things which are displeasing to Him.

We will now make our act of Consecration to the Sacred Heart:

Most Sacred Heart of Jesus, you told Saint Margaret Mary that you would give special blessings to those who honoured your Sacred Heart. We want to give our hearts and lives to you.

We want to do this especially because of your great love for us. You came down from heaven and lived so as to teach us how to please God our Father. When people would not listen to you, you died for us and rose again to teach us that if only we would obey our Father, you would one day lead us to be with you and to be happy with you for ever in your Heavenly Kingdom.

We offer our love to you also, to try to make up for all the times we have said "No" to what God wants of us and because in this way we have been so unlike you who showed us that we should always do the Will of our Father.

Lastly, we offer ourselves to you to try to make up for all those who are wicked and who will not listen to what you want of them. We offer ourselves to you to make up for all the selfishness there is.

Most Sacred Heart of Jesus, we make this offering through our Blessed Lady and Saint Joseph who loved you so much. Help us to love you. Bless and protect us and our homes and school.

185

Most Sacred Heart of Jesus, we put all our trust in you. Take our offering and help us to follow your example.

164. THE COMING OF THE HOLY SPIRIT

V. Come, Holy Spirit, and fill the hearts of your faithful, and kindle in them the fire of your love. Send forth your Spirit and they shall be created.

R. And you will renew the face of the earth.

HYMN

READING

The reading today is from the Acts of the Apostles.

When the day of Pentecost had come, they were all together in one place. And suddenly a sound came from heaven like the rush of a mighty wind, and it filled all the house where they were sitting. And there appeared to them tongues as of fire, distributed and resting on each one of them. And they were all filled with the Holy Spirit and began to speak in other tongues, as the Spirit gave them utterance.

Now there were dwelling in Jerusalem Jews, devout men from every nation under heaven. And at this sound the multitude came together, and they were bewildered, because each one heard them speaking in his own language. And they were amazed and wondered, saying, "Are not all these who are speaking Galileans? And how is it that we hear, each of us in his own native language?

And all were amazed and perplexed, saying to one another, "What does this mean?" But others mocking said, "They are filled with new wine."

But Peter, standing with the eleven, lifted up his voice and addressed them, "Men of Judea and all who dwell in Jerusalem, let this be known to you, and give

186

ear to my words. For these men are not drunk, as you suppose, since it is only the third hour of the day; but this is what was spoken by the prophet Joel:

'And in the last days it shall be, God declares,
that I will pour out my Spirit upon all flesh,
and your sons and your daughters shall prophesy,
and your young men shall see visions,
and your old men shall dream dreams;
yea, and on my menservants and my maidservants
     in those days
I will pour out my Spirit.' "

PRAYER

O God, who has taught the hearts of your faithful by the light of your Holy Spirit, grant that we may be always truly wise and ever rejoice in His consolations, through Christ our Lord. Amen.

THE LORD'S PRAYER

BLESSING

May the peace of God which passes all understanding keep our hearts and minds in the knowledge and the love of God. And may the blessing of God, the Father, the Son, and the Holy Spirit be amongst us and remain with us always. Amen.

165. PETER'S CONVERTS

V. Our help is in the name of the Lord!

R. Who made heaven and earth.

Glory be to the Father. . . .

HYMN

READING

The reading today tells us of many to whom Peter, helped by the Holy Spirit, gave the gift of faith and of how these first Christians lived. It is taken from the Acts of the Apostles.

"Let all the house of Israel therefore know assuredly that God has made him both Lord and Christ, this Jesus whom you crucified."

Now when they heard this they were cut to the heart, and said to Peter and the rest of the apostles, "Brethren, what shall we do?" And Peter said to them, "Repent, and be baptised every one of you in the name of Jesus Christ for the forgiveness of your sins; and you shall receive the gift of the Holy Spirit. For the promise is to you and to your children and to all that are far off, every one whom the Lord our God calls to him." And he testified with many other words and exhorted them, saying, "Save yourselves from this crooked generation." So those who received His word were baptised, and there were added that day about three thousand souls. And they devoted themselves to the apostles' teaching and fellowship, to the breaking of read and the prayers.

YER

F ur hearts and the hearts of all your people with your Holy Sp Lord, so that we may be able to live the kind of lives which will leasing to you. Then we shall be able to share your kingdom you and the Father and the Holy Spirit, world without end. ⟩

THE LOY PRAYER

BLESSING

May the grace Holy Spirit direct our thoughts and help us to learn from Hi honest hearts, now and always. Amen.

166. PET ALS A LAME MAN

V. Blessed be the Holy a Trinity!
R. Now and for evermore.

HYMN

READING

In the Acts of the Apostles, we read how Saint Peter, by the power of the Lord, heals a lame man.

Now Peter and John were going up to the temple at the hour of prayer, the ninth hour. And a man lame from birth was being carried, whom they laid daily at that gate of the temple which is called Beautiful to ask alms of those who entered the temple. Seeing Peter and John about to go into the temple, he asked for alms. And Peter directed his gaze at him, with John, and said, "Look at us." And he fixed his attention upon them, expecting to receive something from them. But Peter said, "I have no silver and gold, but I give you what I have; in the name of Jesus Christ of Nazareth, walk." And he took him by the right hand and raised him up; and immediately his feet and ankles were made strong. And leaping up he stood and walked and entered the temple with them, walking and leaping and praising God. And all the people saw him walking and praising God, and recognized him as the one who sat for alms at the Beautiful Gate of the temple; and they were filled with wonder and amazement at what had happened to him.

PRAYER

Send down on all those who help the sick, O God, the gifts of skill and patience and give to those who are sick help to bear their pains and to accept them by the help of your grace. Through Jesus Christ our Lord. Amen.

THE LORD'S PRAYER

BLESSING

Save us, O God, waking, and guard us sleeping, so that awake we may watch with Christ and asleep we may rest in peace; through Christ our Lord. Amen.

167. PHILIP AND THE ETHIOPIAN

V. O God, come to my assistance!

R. Lord, make haste to help us.

Glory be to the Father. . . .

HYMN

READING

The reading tells us how one of the first people who was not a Jew, wanted to hear more of God. It tells how Philip, by the help of the Holy Spirit, told him of all that Jesus had said and done and how he asked at last that the Holy Spirit come to him in Baptism. The reading is from the Acts of the Apostles.

And the Spirit said to Philip, "Go up and join this chariot." So Philip ran to him, and heard him reading Isaiah the prophet, and asked, "Do you understand what you are reading?" And the Ethiopian said, "How can I, unless some one guides me?" And he invited Philip to come up and sit with him. Now the passage of the scripture which he was reading was this:

"As a sheep led to the slaughter
or a lamb before its shearer is dumb,
so he opens not his mouth.
In his humiliation justice was denied him.
Who can describe his generation?
For his life is taken up from the earth."

And the Ethiopian said to Philip, "About whom, pray, does the prophet say this, about himself or about some one else?" Then Philip opened his mouth, and beginning with this scripture he told him the good news of Jesus. And as they went along the road they came to some water, and the Ethiopian said, "See, here is water! What is to prevent my being baptised?" And he commanded the chariot to stop, and they both went down into the water, Philip and the Ethiopian, and he baptised him.

PRAYER

We thank you for the gift of your Holy Spirit to us in Baptism, O God. Help us to listen to His teachings. Help all those whom you have sent to teach those who do not know you and are waiting to learn about you. Through Christ our Lord. Amen.

THE LORD'S PRAYER

BLESSING

May the grace of our Lord Jesus Christ, and the love of God and the fellowship of the Holy Spirit, be with us all evermore. Amen.

168. ABOVE ALL THINGS
—PRESERVE CHARITY

V. O Lord, open my lips!
R. And my mouth will declare your praise.
 Glory be to the Father. . . .

HYMN

READING

In the reading from the first Epistle of Saint Peter we learn how we should live as good Christians.

The end of all things is at hand; therefore keep sane and sober for your prayers. Above all hold unfailing your love for one another, since love covers a multitude of sins. Practise hospitality ungrudgingly to one another. As each has received a gift, employ it for one another, as good stewards of God's varied grace: whoever speaks, as one who utters oracles of God; whoever renders service, as one who renders it by the strength which God supplies; in order that in everything God may be glorified through Jesus Christ. To him belong glory and dominion for ever and ever.

Amen.

PRAYER

Dear Jesus, help us to love one another. Let us always try to see how we can help others and show our love for you. Amen.

THE LORD'S PRAYER

BLESSING

May the blessing of God the Father, God the Son, and God the Holy Spirit, be amongst us and remain with us always. Amen.

169. BE LOVERS OF THE BRETHREN

V. I have lifted up my eyes to the hills!
R. From whence my help comes.
V. My help comes from the Lord.
R. Who made heaven and earth.
   I confess to Almighty God. . . .

HYMN

READING

The reading today again tells us that the best way in which we can show our love of God is by loving our neighbour. It is from Saint Peter's first Epistle.

Finally, all of you, have unity of spirit, sympathy, love of the brethren, a tender heart and a humble mind. Do not return evil for evil or reviling for reviling; but on the contrary bless, for to this you have been called, that you may obtain a blessing. For
"He that would love life
and see good days,
let him keep his tongue from evil
and his lips from speaking guile;
let him turn away from evil and do right."

PRAYER

Dear Jesus, you have taught us that where there is charity and love, God is present. Please help us never to think any unkind thoughts, say any unkind words or do any unkindness, so that God may be always with us and that we may at last share with Him and you, His only Son, and the Holy Spirit, His everlasting kingdom. Amen.

THE LORD'S PRAYER

BLESSING

May the love of God fill our hearts and minds today and always, through Christ Jesus our Lord. Amen.

170. THE LOAVES AND FISHES

V. Praised be Jesus Christ!
R. Praised for evermore.

HYMN

READING

The reading we are going to hear today is from the Gospel according to Saint Mark. We learn that Jesus will never let us want, especially if we listen to His word.

In those days, when again a great crowd had gathered, and they had nothing to eat, he called his disciples to him, and said to them, "I have compassion on the crowd, because they have been with me now three days, and have nothing to eat; and if I send them away hungry to their homes, they will faint on the way; and some of them have come a long way." And his disciples answered him, "How can one feed these men with bread here in the desert?" And he asked them, "How many loaves have you?" They said, "Seven." And he commanded the crowd to sit down on the ground; and he took the seven loaves, and having given thanks he broke them and gave them to his disciples to set before the people; and they set them before the crowd. And they had a few small fish; and having blessed them, he commanded that these also sould be set before them. And they ate, and were satisfied; and they took up the broken pieces left over, seven baskets full. And there were about four thousand people.

PRAYER

Dear Jesus, we thank you for all the good things you have given us, especially for a share in your life and love and for the food for our souls which is your own Body and Blood which you give us in Holy Communion. We thank you, too, for your words which we hear from the Holy Bible. Help us to listen carefully to them, so that we may be pleasing to our Father in heaven, through Christ our Lord. Amen.

THE LORD'S PRAYER

BLESSING

And now may the God of peace bless all that we do in His name, through Jesus Christ our Lord. Amen.

171. WHO IS MY NEIGHBOUR?

V. O Lord, open my lips!

R. And my mouth will declare your praise.

Glory be to the Father. . . .

HYMN

READING

Saint Luke tells us the story our Lord told when someone asked who his neighbour really was. This story tells of a traveller who is attacked and left to die at the side of the road. Many people saw him and could not be bothered to help him. At last he was helped by a man who was supposed to be an enemy. In helping him this man showed that he really loved him.

And behold, a lawyer stood up to put him to the test, saying, "Teacher, what shall I do to inherit eternal life?" He said to him, "What is written in the law? How do you read?" And he answered "You shall love the Lord your God with all your heart, and with all your soul, and with all your strength, and with all your mind: and your neighbour as yourself."And he said to him, "You have answered right; do this, and you will live."

But he, desiring to justify himself, said to Jesus, "And who is my neighbour?" Jesus replied, "A man was going down from Jerusalem to Jericho, and he fell among robbers, who stripped him and beat him, and departed, leaving him half dead. Now by chance a priest was going down that road; and when he saw him he passed by on the other side. So likewise a Levite, when he came to the place and saw him, passed by on the other side. But a Samaritan, as he journeyed, came to where he was; and when he saw him, he had compassion, and went to him and bound up his wounds, pouring on oil and wine; then he set him on his own beast and brought him to an inn, and took care of him. And the next day he took out two denarii and gave them to the inn-keeper, saying, 'Take care of him; and whatever more you spend, I will repay you when I come back.' Which of these three, do you think, proved neighbour to the man who fell among the robbers?" He said, "The one who showed mercy on him." And Jesus said to him, "Go and do likewise."

PRAYER

O God, help me to realise that I cannot love you unless I love my neighbour. Help me to know that I must show my love by helping anyone who needs help and by never thinking or saying anything which would show I was not loving him. I ask this for the sake of Jesus Christ our Lord. Amen.

THE LORD'S PRAYER

195

H

BLESSING

O God, grant that what we have said with our lips, we may believe in our hearts and do in our lives, to your honour and glory, world without end. Amen.

172. THE GREATEST COMMANDMENT

V. Our help is in the name of the Lord!
R. Who made heaven and earth.
Glory be to the Father. . . .

HYMN

READING

The reading is from the Good News told by Saint Matthew.

But when the Pharisees heard that he had silenced the Sadducees, they came together. And one of them, a lawyer, asked him a question, to test him. "Teacher, which is the great commandment in the law?" And he said to him, "You shall love the Lord your God with all your heart, and with all your soul, and with all your mind. This is the great and first commandment. And a second is like it, you shall love your neighbour as yourself. On these two commandments depend all the law and the prophets."

PRAYER

Before we say the Lord's Prayer, let us think quietly to ourselves how we can best show that we love God and our neighbour today.

(Pause for about half a minute.)

THE LORD'S PRAYER

BLESSING

Bless, guide and strengthen us, your children, and keep us always in your love. Amen.

196

173. THE CHILD SAMUEL

V. O God, come to my assistance!

R. O Lord, make haste to help me.

Glory be to the Father. . . .

HYMN

READING

The reading is from the first book of Samuel.

Now the boy Samuel was ministering to the Lord under Eli. And the word of the Lord was rare in those days; there was no frequent vision.

At that time Eli, whose eyesight had begun to grow dim, so that he could not see, was lying down in his own place; the lamp of God had not yet gone out, and Samuel was lying down within the temple of the Lord, where the ark of God was. Then the Lord called, "Samuel! Samuel!" and he said, "Here I am!" and ran to Eli, and said, "Here I am, for you called me." But he said, "I did not call; lie down again." So he went and lay down. And the Lord called again, "Samuel!" And Samuel arose and went to Eli, and said, "Here I am, for you called me." But he said, "I did not call, my son; lie down again." Now Samuel did not yet know the Lord, and the word of the Lord had not yet been revealed to him. And the Lord called Samuel again the third time. And he arose and went to Eli, and said, "Here I am, for you called me." Then Eli perceived that the Lord was calling the boy. Therefore Eli said to Samuel, "Go, lie down; and if he calls you, you shall say, 'Speak, Lord for thy servant hears.' " So Samuel went and lay down in his place.

And the Lord came and stood forth calling as at other times, "Samuel! Samuel!" And Samuel said, "Speak, for thy servant hears."

And Samuel grew, and the Lord was with him.

PRAYER

Dear Lord, help us to be like the boy Samuel so that we may always listen to the thoughts you give us which tell us what you want us to do, so that we may grow up and that you may be with us always. We ask this for the sake of Jesus Christ your Son our Lord. Amen.

THE LORD'S PRAYER

BLESSING

May the blessing of God Almighty, the Father, the Son and the Holy Spirit, be amongst us and remain with us always. Amen.

174. ASK AND YOU SHALL RECEIVE

V. Our help is in the name of the Lord!
R. Who made heaven and earth.
   I confess to Almighty God. . . .

HYMN

READING

The reading is from the Good News told by Saint Luke.

And I tell you, Ask, and it will be given you; seek, and you will find; knock, and it will be opened to you. For every one who asks receives, and he who seeks finds, and to him who knocks it will be opened. What father among you, if his son asks for a fish, will instead of a fish give him a serpent; or if he asks for an egg, will give him a scorpion? If you then, who are evil, know how to give good gifts to your children, how much more will the heavenly Father give the Holy Spirit to those who ask him!

PRAYER

Dear Lord, help us to know what to ask for so that we may become more like your Son Jesus Christ our Lord who taught us to pray;
Our Father. . . .

198

Lord, give us the blessing never to forget your great love for us and the help always to ask to do your will, for Jesus Christ's sake. Amen.

175. FOR THE SICK

V. Heal your servants, O Lord, who are sick and put their trust in you!
R. Send them help from your holy place.

HYMN

READING

The reading today is from the Epistle of Saint James.

Is any one among you suffering? Let him pray. Is any cheerful? Let him sing praise. Is any among you sick? Let him call for the elders of the church, and let them pray over him, anointing him with oil in the name of the Lord; and the prayer of faith will save the sick man, and the Lord will raise him up; and if he has committed sins, he will be forgiven. Therefore confess your sins to one another, and pray for one another, that you may be healed. The prayer of a righteous man has great power in its effects.

PRAYER

Dear Jesus, you had a special love for those who were sick. Help all those who are sick in our school and parish. Grant that they may soon be better and able to give thanks to you with your people worshipping around your altar. Who lives and reigns, God, world without end. Amen.

THE LORD'S PRAYER

BLESSING

Give your blessing to all the sick and suffering, O Lord, so that they may offer their sorrow up with your sorrows, for the whole world. Amen.

176. FOR VOCATIONS

V. Lord, give us priests and holy priests!

R. Lord, give us priests and holy priests.

Glory be to the Father. . . .

HYMN

READING

The reading is from the letter to the Hebrews.

For every high priest chosen from among men is appointed to act on behalf of men in relation to God, to offer gifts and sacrifices for sins. He can deal gently with the ignorant and wayward, since he himself is beset with weakness. Because of this he is bound to offer sacrifice for his own sins as well as for those of the people. And one does not take the honour upon himself, but he is called by God, just as Aaron was.

So also Christ did not exalt himself to be made a high priest, but was appointed by Him who said to Him,

"Thou art my Son,
today I have begotten thee";

as He says also in another place,

"Thou are a priest for ever,
after the order of Melchizedek."

In the days of His flesh, Jesus offered up prayers and supplications, with loud cries and tears, to Him who was able to save Him from death, and He was heard for His godly fear. Although He was a Son, He learned obedience through what He suffered; and being made perfect He became the source of eternal salvation to all who obey him, being designated by God a high priest after the order of Melchizedek.

PRAYER

Lord, there are many people who cannot have you with them in the Mass and Holy Communion because there are not enough priests.

Please send more and holy priests so that more people may come to know you. Make many boys generous to follow you in this way. Through Jesus Christ our Lord. Amen.

THE LORD'S PRAYER

BLESSING

May the Lord bless us and keep us. May the light of His countenance shine on us and give us His peace, and may the blessing of God, the Father, the Son, and the Holy Spirit be with us all evermore. Amen.

177.   DAVID THE SHEPHERD BOY

V. O Lord, open my lips!

R. And my mouth will declare your praise.

Glory be to the Father. . . .

HYMN

READING

The reading is from the first book of Samuel.

Samuel did what the Lord commanded, and came to Bethlehem. The elders of the city came to meet him trembling, and said, "Do you come peaceably?" And he said, "Peaceably; I have come to sacrifice to the Lord; consecrate yourselves, and come with me to the sacrifice." And he consecrated Jesse and his sons, and invited them to the sacrifice. And Jesse made seven of his sons pass before Samuel. And Samuel said to Jesse, "The Lord has not chosen these." And Samuel said to Jesse, "Are all your sons here?" And he said, "There remains yet the youngest, but behold, he is keeping the sheep." And Samuel said to Jesse, "Send and fetch him; for we will not sit down till he comes here." And he sent, and brought him in. Now he was ruddy, and had beautiful eyes, and was handsome. And the Lord said,

"Arise, anoint him; for this is he." Then Samuel took the horn of oil, and anointed him in the midst of his brothers; and the Spirit of the Lord came mightily upon David from that day forward.

PRAYER

Give us, O God, pure lips and a clean heart as David had. Help us to be true and honest in everything we do. Let us never be mean or spiteful, but teach us to go out of our way to do good. Bless us in our work and in our play that our lives may be full of praise for your honour and glory, through Jesus Christ our Lord. Amen.

THE LORD'S PRAYER

BLESSING

O Lord, bless our going out and our coming in, from this time forth and for evermore. Amen.

178. HOW I LOVE YOUR DWELLING PLACE

V. Praised be Jesus Christ!
R. Praised for ever more!
   Glory be to the Father. . . .

HYMN

READING

Today we are going to listen to one of David's great songs of praise. It is Psalm 84.

How lovely is thy dwelling place,
   O Lord of hosts!
My soul longs, yea, faints
   for the courts of the Lord;

my heart and flesh sing for joy
   to the living God.
Even the sparrow finds a home,
   and the swallow a nest for herself,
   where she may lay her young,
at Thy altars, O Lord of hosts,
   my King and my God.
Blessed are those who dwell in Thy house,
   ever singing Thy praise!
Blessed are the men whose strength is in Thee,
   in whose heart are the highways to Zion.
O Lord God of hosts, hear my prayer;
   give ear, O God of Jacob!
Behold our shield, O God;
   look upon the face of thine anointed!
For a day in Thy courts is better
   than a thousand elsewhere.
I would rather be a doorkeeper in the house of my God
   than dwell in the tents of wickedness.
For the Lord God is a sun and shield;
   He bestows favour and honour.
No good thing does the Lord withhold
   from those who walk uprightly.
O Lord of hosts,
   blessed is the man who trusts in Thee.

PRAYER

Let us think quietly about some of the words of this Psalm and say
a prayer to ourselves.

(*Pause for about half a minute for a silent prayer.*)

THE LORD'S PRAYER

BLESSING

O God, may your blessing and your peace rest on your Church
throughout the whole world for Jesus Christ's sake. Amen.

179. THE DRAUGHT OF FISHES

V. Blessed be the holy and undivided Trinity!
R. Now and for evermore. Amen.

HYMN

READING

The reading is from the Gospel according to Saint Luke.

And He saw two boats by the lake; but the fishermen had gone out of them and were washing their nets. Getting into one of the boats, which was Simon's, He asked him to put out a little from the land. And He sat down and taught the people from the boat. And when He had ceased speaking, He said to Simon, "Put out into the deep and let down your nets for a catch." And Simon answered, "Master, we toiled all night and took nothing! But at your word I will let down the nets." And when they had done this, they enclosed a great shoal of fish; and as their nets were breaking, they beckoned to their partners in the other boat to come and help them. And they came and filled both the boats, so that they began to sink. But when Simon Peter saw it, he fell down at Jesus' knees, saying, "Depart from me, for I am a sinful man, O Lord."

PRAYER

Most merciful Father, give us now the Spirit of your Son Jesus, that He may be with us in the work you have for us during this week, through Jesus Christ our Lord. Amen.

THE LORD'S PRAYER

BLESSING

Bless us O Holy Spirit, with a sincere heart and mind and will, that we may be filled with your power and your peace this day and for evermore. Amen.

180. THE LOVE OF CHRIST COMPELS US

V. O Lord open my lips!

R. And my mouth will declare your praise.

Glory be to the Father. . . .

HYMN

READING

A lot of people have what is called a motto. A motto is a short saying which we can use to help us to remember a rule which is going to help us to behave in a certain way. The motto of the Cubs is "Do your best". The motto of the Brownies is "Lend a hand".

An excellent motto for all boys and girls, whether they are Cubs or Brownies or not is "The love of Christ compels us." This is the motto of many people who try specially to please God.

We should know that God has done so much for us. When we were baptised, He gave us a share of His life. His Love gave us Himself in Holy Communion and, if we have turned away from His Love we have the Sacrament of Penance. He has given us many other graces and blessings.

If we would only think often of what Our Lord has done and keeps on doing, our love for Him would compel or force us to love Him back. Does the Love of Christ force us to love Him back? How can we?

Do we join in the Mass and receive our Lord in Holy Communion because we feel that we are forced to love Him so much that we want to receive Him in Holy Communion?

Do we make our morning offering each day because we feel we really must offer to Christ all that we think or say or do? Do we do all that we can to help the sick, the poor, the Missions?

Each day we should try to have a few moments when we can be quiet and on our own and we should use that quiet time to think of something Our Lord has done for us. That will make us want to do something for Our Lord.

It would be a good idea to say to ourselves each morning "The Love of Christ compels us." If we do that, we will find that we are doing many things for the Love of Christ.

Try to make this your motto: "The Love of Christ compels us."

PRAYER

Lord Jesus Christ, teach us to show our love for you by always being kind to all the boys and girls and grown ups that we meet. Help us never to say an unkind thing to them or about them. We ask this because you came to lead us all to our heavenly Father and because you showed us such great love by offering your life for us on the cross. So may we be always pleasing to you, who live and reign with the Father and the Holy Spirit, world without end. Amen.

THE LORD'S PRAYER

BLESSING

Bless us, O Lord, and all those we see or speak with today. Amen.

181. THE BURNING BUSH

V. O Lord, open my lips!

R. And my lips will declare your praise.

Glory be to the Father. . . .

HYMN

READING

The reading today tells of how Moses saw the burning bush and how God showed himself to Moses and made him leader of the people. It is from the book of Exodus.

Now Moses was keeping the flock of his father-in-law, Jethro, the priest of Midian; and he led his flock to the west side of the wilderness, and came to Horeb, the mountain of God. And the angel of the Lord appeared to him in a flame of fire out of the midst of a bush; and he looked, and lo, the bush was burning, yet it was not consumed. And Moses said, "I will turn aside and see this great sight, why the bush is not burnt."

When the Lord saw that he turned aside to see, God called to him out of the bush, "Moses, Moses!" And he said, "Here am I." Then He said, "Do not come near; put off your shoes from your feet, for the place on which you are standing is holy ground." And He said, "I am the God of your father, the God of Abraham, the God of Isaac, and the God of Jacob." And Moses hid his face, for he was afraid to look at God.

Then the Lord said, "I have seen the affliction of my people who are in Egypt, and have heard their cry because of their taskmasters; I know their sufferings, and I have come down to deliver them out of the hand of the Egyptians, and to bring them up out of that land to a good and broad land, a land flowing with milk and honey."

PRAYER

We thank you, Lord, for making yourself known to Moses and for choosing a people to learn your ways so that at last you could send your only Son to lead us back to share the life and love of our heavenly Father. Help us to know and love you more and more, through Jesus Christ our Lord, who lives and reigns with you and the Holy Spirit, world without end. Amen.

THE LORD'S PRAYER

BLESSING

To God the Father, God the Son, and God the Holy Spirit, be glory and praise for evermore. Amen.

182. THE FOOLISH GIRLS

V. O God, come to my assistance!

R. Lord, make haste to help me.

Glory be to the Father. . . .

HYMN

READING

Saint Matthew tells us of some foolish girls who were supposed to be getting ready for the bridegroom at a wedding. They were so happy about the wedding that they were not ready for him when he arrived. We are supposed to be getting ready for when our Lord will come again in glory—for when we meet Him. Are we really bothering to get ready? Listen to the story from the Gospel according to Saint Matthew.

Then the kingdom of heaven shall be compared to ten maidens who took their lamps and went to meet the bridegroom. Five of them were foolish, and five were wise. For when the foolish took their lamps, they took no oil with them; but the wise took flasks of oil with their lamps. As the bridegroom was delayed, they all slumbered and slept. But at midnight there was a cry, 'Behold, the bridegroom! Come out to meet him.' Then all those maidens rose and trimmed their lamps. And the foolish said to the wise, 'Give us some of your oil, for our lamps are going out.' But the wise replied, 'Perhaps there will not be enough for us and for you; go rather to the dealers and buy for yourselves.' And while they went to buy, the bridegroom came, and those who were ready went in with him to the marriage feast; and the door was shut. Afterward the other maidens came also, saying, 'Lord, lord, open to us.' But he replied, 'Truly, I say to you, I do not know you.' Watch therefore for you know neither the day nor the hour.

PRAYER

O God, help us always to be ready for your coming so that when the time comes for us to meet you face to face, we will be able to be with you and to praise you and be happy with you forever in your kingdom, through Christ our Lord. Amen.

THE LORD'S PRAYER

BLESSING

May God the Father bless us; may Christ His Son defend us and may His Holy Spirit comfort us now and forever. Amen.

183. THE VISITATION

V. Blessed art thou among women!

R. And blessed is the fruit of thy womb, Jesus!

HYMN

READING

Today is the feast of the Visitation of our Lady. Saint Luke tells us how our blessed Lady went to visit her cousin Saint Elizabeth, who was going to have a baby who was to be John the Baptist. Elizabeth knew as soon as she saw our Lady that she too was going to have a baby and that her baby was to be the Lord.

"Mary rose up and went with all haste to a town of Juda, in the hill country to the house of Zechariah and greeted Elizabeth. And when Elizabeth heard the greeting of Mary, the babe leaped in her womb; and Elizabeth was filled with the Holy Spirit and she exclaimed with a loud cry, 'Blessed are you among women, and blessed is the fruit of your womb! And why is this granted me, that the mother of my Lord should come to me? For behold, when the voice of your greeting came to my ears, the babe in my womb leaped for joy. And blessed is she who believed that there would be fulfilment of what was spoken to her from the Lord.' And Mary said: 'My soul magnifies the Lord; my spirit has found joy in God who is my Saviour.' "

PRAYER

Grant to us, O Lord, the gift of your heavenly grace so that we for whom salvation was begun by our Lady's great "Yes" to God, may come closer to Him, and praise Him, and love Him forever with our Blessed Lady, through Jesus Christ our Lord. Amen.

THE LORD'S PRAYER

BLESSING

May the love of our blessed Lady get for us a great love and many blessings from her Son, Jesus Christ our Lord. Amen.

184. VARIETIES OF GIFTS

V. Blessed be the Holy and Undivided Trinity!
R. Now and for evermore. Amen.

HYMN

READING

Today's reading is from Saint Paul's first letter to the people of Corinth. In it he tells us that there are many kinds of gifts which God has given to us and that we should remember that whatever gifts we may have come to us from God's love for us in the Holy Spirit.

Now there are varieties of gifts, but the same Spirit. To one is given through the Spirit the utterance of wisdom, and to another the utterance of knowledge according to the same Spirit, to another faith by the same Spirit, to another gifts of healing by the one Spirit, to another the working of miracles, to another prophecy, to another the ability to distinguish between spirits, to another various kinds of tongues, to another the interpretation of tongues. All these are inspired by one and the same Spirit, who apportions to each one individually as he wills.

PRAYER

O God, who has made us all different and has given to each of us the special gifts which we have, help us to use these talents while we are still at school. Grant that we may use our talents for your honour and glory through Jesus Christ our Lord. Amen.

THE LORD'S PRAYER

BLESSING

To you, O Lord, be all praise and honour now and forever more. Amen.

185. THE SERMON ON THE MOUNT

V. I have lifted up my eyes to the hills!

R. From whence my help comes.

V. My help comes from the Lord.

R. Who made heaven and earth.

I confess to Almighty God. ...

HYMN

READING

The Sermon on the Mount tells us the chief ways there are of showing our love for God and our neighbour. If we listen to what our Lord has to say to us here and try to do the things He tells us we shall be able to share His kingdom. The reading is from the Gospel according to Saint Matthew.

Seeing the crowds, He went up on the mountain, and when He sat down His disciples came to Him. And He opened His mouth and taught them, saying:

"Blessed are the poor in spirit, for theirs is the kingdom of heaven.

"Blessed are those who mourn, for they shall be comforted.

"Blessed are the meek, for they shall inherit the earth.

"Blessed are those who hunger and thirst for righteousness, for they shall be satisfied.

"Blessed are the merciful, for they shall obtain mercy.

"Blessed are the pure in heart, for they shall see God.

"Blessed are the peacemakers, for they shall be called sons of God.

"Blessed are those who are persecuted for righteousness' sake, for theirs is the kingdom of heaven.

"Blessed are you when men revile you and persecute you and utter all kinds of evil against you falsely on my account. Rejoice and be glad, for your reward is great in heaven, for so men persecuted the prophets who were before you."

PRAYER

Give us ears, good Lord, to hear the wonderful words you spoke. Help us to listen carefully to what has been read and to choose one way at least in which we can be specially blessed by you, for Jesus Christ's sake. Amen.

THE LORD'S PRAYER

BLESSING

May the Lord bless us and keep us from all that is wrong and bring us to life everlasting. Through Christ our Lord. Amen.

186. WHO IS THE GREATEST?

V. Praised be Jesus Christ!
R. Praised for evermore.
   Glory be to the Father. . . .

HYMN

READING

In Saint Matthew's Good News, we learn that the greatest in God's kingdom are those who are even willing to suffer for our Lord. We can perhaps do this best by really putting ourselves out to help all those who are in need and helping those we do not like very much.

At that time the disciples came to Jesus, saying, "Who is the greatest in the kingdom of heaven?" And calling to Him a child, He put him in the midst of them, and said, "Truly, I say to you, unless you turn and become like children, you will never enter the kingdom of heaven. Whoever humbles himself like this child, he is the greatest in the kingdom of heaven.

"Whoever receives one such child in my name receives me; but whoever causes one of these little ones who believe in me to sin, it would be better for him to have a great millstone fastened round his neck and to be drowned in the depth of the sea."

PRAYER

O Lord, help us always to be simple and child-like and to do at once what we know you want us to do without thinking about what other people may say of us. Give us the strength to do this with the help of your Holy Spirit, who lives and reigns world without end. Amen.

THE LORD'S PRAYER

BLESSING

May the blessing of God, the Father, the Son, and the Holy Spirit, be with us now and always. Amen.

187. THE TRUE VINE

V. O Lord, open my lips!

R. And my mouth will declare your praise.

Glory be to the Father. . . .

HYMN

READING

The story our Lord tells in the Gospel according to Saint John shows us that we should always stay true to our Lord if we are to have a share of our Father's kingdom.

"I am the true vine, and my Father is the vine-dresser. Every branch of mine that bears no fruit, he takes away, and every branch that does bear fruit he prunes that it may bear more fruit. I am the vine, you are the branches. He who abides in me, and I in him, he it is that bears much fruit, for apart from me you can do nothing. If you abide in me, and my words abide in you, ask whatever you will, and it shall be done for you. By this my Father is glorified, that you bear much fruit, and so prove to be my disciples. As the Father has loved me, so have I loved you; abide in my love. If you keep my commandments, you will abide in my love, just as I have kept my Father's commandments and abide in His love. These things I have spoken to you, that my joy may be in you, and that your joy may be full.

"This is my commandment, that you love one another as I have loved you. Greater love has no man than this, that a man lay down his life for his friends. You are my friends if you do what I command you."

PRAYER

O God, you love us so much. Help us to be patient with the faults we see in others because we probably have even greater faults. May we be merciful to others as we hope that you will be merciful

214

to us. Help us to follow your teachings and always remain true
to the church which you came to give to the world. Through Jesus
Christ our Lord. Amen.

THE LORD'S PRAYER

BLESSING

O Lord, forgive what we have been. Make us holy and help us to
do all things for you. Amen.

188. SAINT JOHN THE BAPTIST

V. Lamb of God, who takes on himself the sins of the world.

R. Have mercy on us!

HYMN

READING

St. John the Baptist was the cousin of our Lord. He
was specially chosen by God to prepare the people for
our Lord's teaching.

He was a prophet—someone who speaks out God's
message. The message St. John has for us is that we
should pray and do penance.

Our Lord tells us that we should pray always. We
do this if we offer all that we think or say or do to God
our Father. Do we offer Him these things each morning
in our morning offering? Do we remember during the
day what we have offered to God?

St. John showed us by his example that we should
do penance to be ready for the time when we are called
to God our Father in Heaven. Do you ever do anything
for God which in your selfishness you would rather not
do? Like going to bed as soon as you are told instead
of grumbling and asking to stay up a bit longer to watch
the next television programme? Do you ever make an
effort to go to Mass, say, on a Saturday morning or pay
a visit to the Blessed Sacrament?

St. John showed us also how to be strong in faith. He went to prison and was put to death because he chose the things of God rather than the things of men.

Ask God to give you a strong faith and to help you by your faith to draw other people to Him.

PRAYER

Dear Lord, help us to listen to the message of Saint John the Baptist and to do our little acts of penance so that we may be ready to take our place in your heavenly kingdom, through Jesus Christ our Lord. Amen.

THE LORD'S PRAYER

BLESSING

May the blessing of God, the Father, the Son and the Holy Spirit, be with us now and always. Amen.

189. SAINT PAUL

V. Our help is in the name of the Lord!

R. Who made heaven and earth.

Glory be to the Father.

HYMN

READING

Saint Paul was a very clever Jew who hated Christ and the first Christians. He learned, in a great vision, when he was on his way to Damascus to persecute the Christians there, that Jesus was the Saviour who had been promised to the world to lead all men back to their heavenly Father.

He was baptised and after praying hard he tried to make up for all that he had done wrong by teaching others the great love of our Lord. With the other Apostles he never tired of showing both the Jews and other people too that Jesus had come and died and risen again so that if we followed His teaching we, too, would rise again and have a place in God's heavenly kingdom.

Saint Paul was a great missioner who travelled thousands of miles to bring people to the love of God. When he had visited a place and started the church there, he left priests behind to say Mass and to give the Sacraments. He wrote long letters to the people he had brought to Christ. These letters tell us now how we ought to be good Christians. They are often read in church because God used Saint Paul to give his message to us all.

Let us ask Saint Paul to pray for all those who are trying to spread the word of God in our own country and all over the world. Let us ask him to pray for us that we may be sorry for any sins that we have done. Let us ask him to help us to make up for all the times we have said "No" to God by doing something which will bring other people to know our Lord, and to love Him and serve Him.

PRAYER

O God, who taught many people by the preaching of Saint Paul, your Apostle, grant that we may enjoy his prayers for us. Through our Lord Jesus Christ, your Son, who lives and reigns with You and the Holy Spirit, world without end. Amen.

THE LORD'S PRAYER

BLESSING

O God, may your blessing rest on us and on all that we do in your Name, for Jesus Christ's sake. Amen.

190. WHAT MUST I DO TO GET TO HEAVEN?

V. O God, come to my assistance!
R. Lord, make haste to help me.
    Glory be to the Father. . . .

HYMN

READING

One day a man asked our Lord what he must do to have a share in His kingdom. Our Lord told him that he should keep the laws that God, in His goodness, had given to us. Let us listen to what our Lord had to say in the Good News told by Saint Luke.

And a ruler asked Him, "Good Teacher, what shall I do to inherit eternal life?" And Jesus said to him, "Why do you call me good? No one is good but God alone. You know the commandments: 'Do not commit adultery, Do not kill, Do not steal, Do not bear false witness, Honour your father and mother.' " And he said, "All these I have observed from my youth." And when Jesus heard it, he said to him, "One thing you still lack. Sell all that you have and distribute to the poor, and you will have treasure in heaven; and come, follow me."

PRAYER

Dear Lord, you have called us to worship you. Help us to be good enough to get to heaven. Make us strong to do what you want us to do and let us think more of what you want us to do than of what we want to do, for Jesus Christ's sake. Amen.

THE LORD'S PRAYER

BLESSING

May the Holy Spirit direct our thoughts and help us to learn of Him with honest hearts, now and always. Amen.

191. THE LORD IS MY SHEPHERD

V. O Lord, open my lips!
R. And my mouth will declare your praise.
   Glory be to the Father. . . .

HYMN

READING

The reading today is Psalm 23. It tells us that God will look after us always and that if we follow our

Shepherd He will take us safely to His kingdom in heaven.

> The Lord is my shepherd, I shall not want;
>   He makes me lie down in green pastures.
> He leads me beside still waters;
>   He restores my soul.
> He leads me in paths of righteousness
>   for His name's sake.
> Even though I walk through the valley of the
>   shadow of death,
>   I fear no evil;
> for Thou art with me;
>   Thy rod and Thy staff,
>   they comfort me.
> Thou preparest a table before me
>   in the presence of my enemies;
> Thou anointest my head with oil,
>   my cup overflows.
> Surely goodness and mercy shall follow me
>   all the days of my life;
> and I shall dwell in the house of the Lord
>   for ever.

PRAYER

O God, who by the example of the Good Shepherd shows us the way to heaven, grant that we may not only follow His example but that we may also be examples to those who are around us. Grant this for the sake of Jesus Christ your Son who lives and reigns with you and the Holy Spirit, one God, world without end. Amen.

THE LORD'S PRAYER

BLESSING

May the Lord bless us and keep us. May the light of His countenance shine on us and give us His peace now and always. Amen.

192. SAINT MARY MAGDALENE

V. Blessed be the Holy and Undivided Trinity!

R. Now and for ever more. Amen.

HYMN

READING

Saint Mary Magdalene is one of the great saints we read about in the Gospels.

Mary Magdalene had been a great hater of Almighty God and a very selfish person who always wanted her own pleasure and so she said a many great "No's" to God.

But even though she was a great sinner, our Lord loved her and was always waiting for her to turn to love Him and to turn from her sins. At last Mary began to see how sinful she was and began to love our Lord. One day she went in a house to see our Lord when He was with some friends and she cried because she had committed so many sins. Some of our Lord's friends were very surprised when they saw that He was friendly to her when she had been well known as a sinner. But He told them that He had forgiven her now because she was sorry and because she now loved Him so much.

Mary Magdalene never forgot how she had displeased our Lord and she continued to love Him more and more. When our Lord was crucified she was with our Lady and Saint John near the cross. When our Lord rose from the dead Mary Magdalene was the first person our Lord showed Himself to and He sent her to tell the good news of His Resurrection to the Apostles.

We learn from Saint Mary Magdalene that God will always forgive our sins no matter how bad they are, if we are sorry for them. He will give us the grace to love Him if only we ask for it.

We should ask Saint Mary Magdalene to pray that

we may learn to love God more with all our hearts and minds.

Saint Mary Magdalene, pray for us that we may learn to love our Lord as much as you did.

PRAYER

O Lord Jesus Christ, grant that through the prayers of Saint Mary Magdalene, we may learn to love you and to be really sorry for our sins. Through the same Jesus Christ, our Lord who lives and reigns with the Father and the Holy Spirit, one God, world without end. Amen.

THE LORD'S PRAYER

BLESSING

May the blessing of God, the Father, the Son, and the Holy Spirit, be with us all evermore. Amen.

193. END OF YEAR SERVICE

V. My help is in the name of the Lord!
R. Who made heaven and earth.
  I confess to Almighty God. . . .

HYMN

READING

The first reading is from Psalm 1.

Blessed is the man
  who walks not in the counsel of the wicked,
nor stands in the way of sinners,
  nor sits in the seat of scoffers;
but his delight is in the law of the Lord,
  and on his law he meditates day and night.
He is like a tree
  planted by streams of water,

that yields its fruit in its season,
and its leaf does not wither.
In all that he does, he prospers,
for the Lord knows the way of the righteous,
but the way of the wicked will perish.

HYMN OF THANKSGIVING

READING

Now we are going to read from Psalm 119, telling
God that we will remember His loving law which He
has given to us, to keep us close to Him.

With my whole heart I seek Thee;
let me not wander from Thy commandments!
I have laid up Thy word in my heart,
that I might not sin against Thee.
I will meditate on Thy precepts,
and fix my eyes on Thy ways.
I will delight in Thy statutes;
I will not forget Thy word.
Deal bountifully with Thy servant,
that I may live and observe Thy word.

PRAYER

Look down on us as we gather here on the last day of the school
year, O Lord. May those of us who are leaving remember what
they have learned in their lessons, in the playground and in their
games. Let them remember their friends amongst the teachers and
children. May we all be faithful to your loving laws. We thank you
for all the blessings you have given us during this year at ....
.... School. Protect us during the holidays. Help us to
do something for you during the holidays by doing something which
will help our neighbour, so that we may be well pleasing to you.
Through Christ our Lord. Amen.

THE LORD'S PRAYER

BLESSING

O God, may your blessing rest on us and all that we do for your
sake, now and for evermore. Amen.